Expert Skiing

This was the top. I had come by a long couloir, narrow under the summit but running down onto broad snow fields carved with rolling pitches, down into clumps of scrub trees and finally to the pine forest of the valley floor.

This was the highest peak in the area, but as I had climbed so had the giants climbed, in the distance, shouldering their way into the sky, standing now in a great white audience around me. There was an ache in my heart. Call it discovery, or rediscovery. Something I'd forgotten—the wind stirring among the rocks, or the brilliance of a desert sky over a range, or the pull of all that distance.

Here it was corn snow, just softening up.

I laced my boots, stretching the leather tightly around my feet, then carefully strapped on my skis. Water was beginning to trickle from the cracks in the rocks. It was spring down in the valleys. There was a mile of gravity pulling at my feet.

Poles on, a quick jump, I started down . . . .

. . . But where did this run really begin? It began at the beginning, with learning to ski.

Expert Skiing

DAVID BRADLEY

RALPH MILLER

ALLISON MERRILL

GROSSET & DUNLAP, Inc.   *Publishers*

NEW YORK

To Dr. Ralph Miller, Josephine Bradley, and
Shirley Merrill.

Preface

This is a book about skiing. No book could hope to cover the whole range of the sport: the problems of learning, the skills of proficiency, the special techniques of racing, the variety of recreational skiing. But we will try to touch on them all. We will try to open the doors.

It is not a book for beginners only. There have been many such. We begin at the beginning, but do not propose to stay there. The elements of good ski technique are described in a simplified way, not as an end in themselves but as a way of aiming the beginner in the right direction. After that come the refinements of style—the Modern Technique and its variations—which enable the skier to ski *to the best of his ability.*

Most skiers hold a secret image of themselves skiing freely, with French élan and Austrian control, down any kind of terrain. It is a good image to have. The purpose of this book is to help each skier approach as nearly as he can that ideal.

But skiing is a "feeling," a sense of poise governing the relationship between a person, his skis, the side of a mountain, and the pull of gravity. It is not an intellectual exercise, or the mastery of a technique, or a race against time (or old age), or even just a sport.

Much less is skiing a book. You will have to discover these feelings for yourself: the solid bite of edges on ice, the sweep of a well-carved turn, the rhythm of mambo, the hot joyous muscular feeling of running across country, the sense of riding the air over a jumping hill, the yearning upward of touring which takes you by many discoveries into the heart of winter mountains.

The beginner can shorten his learning period many weeks by putting himself in the hands of a good instructor. Yet rare are instructors still, and rarer any who have time for more than beginnings. The finer points that lead to excellence have to be picked up by imitation, or word of mouth, or suffering experience, and so are the fit subjects for a book.

Study the book. Leaf through it, looking at the pictures, as you are bound to do; but then go back and read. There is a logical sequence to the subjects covered. Compare what you are doing on skis with what the pictures show. Study the serial pictures for one action at a time: how the skis turn; how the edges grip; how the feet work together; how the knees, hips, shoulders, arms follow their own necessary sequences. You will be surprised how much you can see if you dissect a single motion in this way.

This book should be approached actively, tested, enjoyed, lived in. The "feel" of skiing will come as your skill increases. Whatever you discover in these many pages and hundreds of photographs will be yours for good when built into muscle and bone, rhythm and confidence.

Ralph Miller
Al Merrill
Dave Bradley

Contents

Acknowledgements

Anyone writing a new book on skiing owes a debt to those who have blazed the way before: Proctor, Schniebs, Prager, Lunn, Lang, Bergsland, Joubert and many others. In one way or another our obligations could be traced back more than a hundred years, but this would be tedious and unnecessary. With this book we, the authors, simply join those who love the sport of skiing so much they feel they must help to pass it on.

Yet special help came to us like windfalls and for that we gratefully give special thanks: to *Gene Vance* for taking almost all the sequence pictures in the large alpine section of the book; to *Richard Eliot* for his photos on cross-country running; to *Don Cutter* for his Robot camera; to *Dave McCoy* for his mountain and to *Emil Rueb,* photographer extraordinary, of Hanover, N.H., whose patience in meeting our excessive demands was only exceeded by his skill in printing.

For help in collecting the large photographs:
Dorice Taylor of the Sun Valley News Bureau
Margaret Durrance of Aspen
Fred Berko of Aspen
Wolfgang Lert of Los Angeles
Joern Gerdts of Salt Lake City
Hanson Carroll of Norwich, Vt.
Adrian Bouchard of Hanover
Bill Eldred, and *Ski Magazine,* of Hanover
David Brower of the Sierra Club of California
James Laughlin of New Directions, Norfolk, Conn.
Harold, Richard, Stephen, and William Bradley

For enthusiastic assistance from abroad:
Hans Truöl of Sonthofen all Gau, Germany
Einar Bergsland, and "På Ski," Oslo, Norway
Heinrich Clausing of Garmisch, Germany
Manfred Dressel and Secy. Schröder of the Deutscher Skiläufer-Verband, Berlin, Germany
Pauli Swanljung and O. A. Gottleben of the Suomen Hiihtoliitto, Helsinki, Finland
Walter Studer of Bern, Switzerland
'Comet' & Co. of Zürich, Switzerland
Hans Steiner of St. Moritz, Switzerland
And Georges Joubert of France, whose study and analysis of today's racing champions have to a large extent defined the movements of the modern technique in skiing.

For the translations into English of our struggles with paper:
Ruth Quinn of Hanover and Karin Schriever of Lyme, N.H.
Jennie Wells of West Lebanon, N.H.
Louanna Smith of Concord, N.H.

And to Mrs. R. E. Miller, Shirley Merrill, and Elisabeth Bradley who fed us, waited, watched, groaned, edited, tended babies, dogs, cats, shared our frustrations and (we hope) our convictions about this book.

Expert Skiing

"Skiing is only a way of walking or sliding on snow. . .

Learning to Ski

Skiing is easy to learn. It is, after all, only a way of walking or sliding on snow, with gravity doing much of the work. Elongated wooden shoes have been in use for thousands of years. Long before skiing became a sport or a fashionable something-to-do, it was a necessity among winter-bound peoples. No one knows how long. There is a pair of skis in a Scandinavian museum that date from an age twice as remote as the songs of Homer. Meanwhile the gods of our era loom large—Toni Sailer, Hannes Schneider, Dick Durrance, Sigmund Ruud—but the gods, too, once had to learn.

And they learned under far less favorable conditions. Skiing is easier now than ever before: ski boots are well designed; the skis themselves are miracles of wood and plastic engineering; there are good ski instructors and ski schools; there are ski slopes of all kinds, laid out and grassed and groomed as carefully as a golf course; there are lifts to take you up so that you can run down 10,000 or 15,000 or even 20,000 vertical feet in a single day.

Getting
Started
But first things first: before you can slide, you must walk; before you can let your skis run, you must know how to stop them. This chapter deals with the controls: walking, sliding, turning, stopping—the fundamentals which every skier must know. It will also serve as a reminder for those who already ski. At the beginning of the season even the expert needs to begin again; he must let his body remember how to ski, how to move, how to relax, how the snow feels and how to carve a turn in it.

The beginner and the expert alike, in the first days of winter, would be well advised just to go out and ski, shunning all uphill mechanisms until the slippery planks seem natural and the body sure of its balance.

If you are a beginner, you will have to know a few basic things about equipment before you start out. In the Appendix is a full discussion of equipment, both recreational and racing.

This much deserves to be emphasized here:
1. Good boots are more important than good skis.
2. Beginner's skis should be short, no higher than the person's height. Learning the fundamentals of skiing may be lengthened from two weeks to two years if you use skis that are too long and heavy.
3. Poles should reach to your armpits.
4. Safety bindings are well worth the cost, provided you learn how to keep them in accurate adjustment.

Properly equipped, you will be surprised how easy and natural it is to ski. Easier by far than learning to swim. There is no peril here for the beginner if he treats gravity with respect and learns one step well before going on to the next.

Children learn to ski in a few days. They have a natural grace, very little momentum, and no great distance to fall. They put on their skis and forget about them. Unruffled by advice, unaware of spectators, they ski by eye and instinct. But adults have to learn. They are accustomed to being taught. They worry about how they "look." They need books and instructors, pictures, explanations, practice. Most of all they need confidence.

If you are a beginner, or if you are getting your ski legs back at the beginning of the season, it may help if you remember that from the first steps on, you "are skiing." There are several million skiers today. Half of them are still learning what is in this chapter—the fundamentals. But they are all skiing. They may prefer to call it "learning," as though skiing were something else to be discovered tomorrow. Everyone feels that way, including the best racers who say that they are "training."

You will learn, but don't make work of it—enjoy it. Start with walking. Set your bindings in a loose position and just go off walking and sliding cross country. Get used to the feel of the seemingly clumsy things, the way they spring on the bumps, the way they hold a straight line, the way the edges grip. Learn how to use your poles for propulsion as well as balance, incorporating the rhythm of your arms into the rhythm of your feet. Learn to move by sliding your skis forward instead of lifting them. Pick a gentle pasture and let your skis carry you down over the undulations of the snow and out on the flat. Side step up again, making your edges bite. Run the slope again, flexing and straightening your body with the bumps. Try traversing obliquely down the slope, holding your direction by means of your uphill edges.

There is no need to do more than this during the first few days. This is skiing. Let yourself get acquainted with snow and woods and hills. They will not be obstacles very long, but friends worthy of a life-time association.

When your skis have taught you this much, you will be tempted to go straightway to a ski area and start for the top. Resist the temptation just a little longer. Instead, try the special exercises given in the picture section of this chapter. Their purpose is not to "get you in shape." They are to acquaint you with the positions and actions your body will be using in skiing. Learn them—learn to feel them—while standing on a flat, untroubled by motion and the panicky necessity of having to turn or stop or fall. The positions and actions described here will seem odd at first and perhaps exaggerated. Nevertheless let your body know them well; it will use them well later on.

When at last you do make your entrée into the ski-tow culture, be a little choosy still. It is not yet time to try the Expert Trail. Use a gentler slope with a smooth flat outrun at the bottom, wide enough and free enough of people to maneuver in. Take the snow when or where it is right, neither porcelain-hard nor heavy with deep new snow. Your next steps will be easy if the conditions are favorable, and your next steps will make you a competent skier; did you know that? Did you know that with a *kick turn,* a *snowplow turn,* and a *sideslip* you can negotiate almost any slope you will ever be on?

Learn these basic maneuvers accurately; you will use them the rest of your life. *Practice only one thing at a time and make a habit of doing that one thing precisely:* heels together, knees together, standing well, walking and sliding with a clean rhythm, even carrying your skis—like a skier. The habit will help you immeasurably later on. The sloppy skier who sloughs out on a slope and ties weary slats onto wornout boots is not likely to be—unless he is a comic artist—the one you next see flowing down the slope in a swish "mambo."

Kick turns, snowplow (or "stem") *turns, sideslips*—they have such impressive and ominous titles! They are and will always be the fundamental controls in skiing, but they are not difficult to learn if your skis are reasonably short and the snow fresh packed. Children literally invent these maneuvers for themselves as they go along. Without instruction or explanations they fall into using them quite naturally and they use them perfectly almost at once, for children accept the skis as part of their bodies and concentrate all their attention on the slope ahead.

The pictures given in the latter part of this chapter will help you understand these simple techniques for controlling your speed and direction: how to cross a hill obliquely, how to make your edges bite or slide, how to drift sideways downhill, how to turn. Study the pictures in detail. Follow the sequence of motions the skis go through, then the knees, hips, shoulders, arms, poles. In the same way analyze the turns that other people are making. And analyze your own.

In the end you must be your own instructor, learning to feel what you are doing that is right or wrong. Ask yourself such questions as these: Was I sitting back too much? Or stiff-legged? Did I depend too much on the inside ski, leaning into the hill? Were my knees really tight together? Were my knees and hips working in a relaxed way? A good pianist feels the music in his finger tips. In time you will learn to feel skiing from the tips of your poles to the bite of your edges.

The *kick turn* and *snowplow turn* are finished actions in themselves. You will use them all your life. The *sideslip* is both a necessary method of controlling speed and the basis of other turns and techniques which come with higher speed. So do not hurry through these fundamentals. With these steps half learned you could probably get down most ski trails—scraping, bouncing, fighting all the way. But you will never become an expert skier in that fashion. Learn—and perfect—these steps on a gentle slope away from the traffic of pelting bodies.

The *sideslip* will cause you some difficulty. Yet it must be learned properly for it is an essential part of almost every turning or checking action in good skiing. It is the first step in learning to make your edges work for you—"edge control" as the experts call it.

First is the sideslip without forward motion. Standing with your skis together and horizontal, you will try, by lessening the bite of the uphill edges, to make your skis drift sideways downhill. When you discover that this is possible, you will also find that by varying the bite of the edges you can drift slowly or fast or stop. When you can manage your skis sliding in this way down the fall line (straight down the hill), then, by shifting your weight forward or back a little, you can make the skis drift obliquely backward or forward.

It sounds difficult? Not if the conditions are favorable. On flat hills, or in rough-packed snow or slush it may be impossible for you, for there will not be enough pull of gravity to set your skis sliding. But take courage, pick out a slope steeper than any you are used to skiing on. Preferably one packed smooth but not icy. Better still try it on a hard-packed hill that has an inch or two of fresh snow dusted over it. Your skis will slip easily and show you, in their marks on the snow, the record of your mistakes and accomplishments.

Falls are not a breach of social etiquette; they are unavoidable, and necessary, and good. They are part of the learning process and, indeed, in certain emergency situations a fall is the best way to stop.

Falling

Trouble comes when you fight a fall too long, changing an easy slithering skid into a real crash. Children never fall that way. They fall naturally because they understand that it is natural to fall. Unaware of others looking on, they feel no humiliation in falling. They simply relax, slide, get up and go on, never giving the matter another thought. And so children almost never get hurt.

Certain rules you should know. They will help keep you out of trouble:
1. Keep your knees and skis together. (A spread-eagle fall is the worst.)
2. Don't fight the fall too long. Pick out a comfortable spot and plan to fall there.
3. Fall backwards and to one side.
4. Relax.

Deep soft snow is probably the most dangerous snow for the beginner. It tends to lock the skis in a spread-out position and pitch the skier forward. Patchy ice or half-broken snow and sharp bumps (moguls) will also guarantee you much practice in falling until you have learned to anticipate what they will do to you. In such conditions you must be especially conscious of what your knees and skis are doing.

Getting up again is a simple matter of maneuvering your feet, or rolling over beetle-like, until your skis are horizontal and below you on the slope.

The pictures which follow illustrate these fundamentals. They are not exaggerated postures intended to overemphasize some point, but rather sequences (taken with a Robot camera, eight frames per second) which analyze the ordinary motions that an expert makes in skiing.

Tying skis for carrying.

The fun grows with the skill.

Precision in skiing should become a habit even in the simplest things — standing, walking, climbing, dressing, handling skis.

Before sliding come standing and walking. Remember?

Practice them. Can you see the difference between a careless stance and a correct one? Trivial? Not at all. You have to know the feeling of having your knees and feet and skis always working together.

Being relaxed is as important as being precise. It is not the same as being sloppy. In the right-hand pictures the skier practices locking the skis together as he would in a turn.

Study the body components *separately*. The skis, the feet, the knees, the carriage of the body.

How much can your ankles bend in a tight boot?

The amount is important, for the ankle is the joint between you and your skis. Your weight, your balance, your turns need both strength and flexibility at this joint.

If you cannot bend this far, loosen the tops of your boots until they are more broken in. The heel of the boot should remain on the ski.

Stiff ankles cause one to bend too much from the waist or to sit back placing the center of gravity behind the feet.

Try walking without poles. First short steps, then longer ones.

Remember to slide your skis on the snow; don't lift them. Slide them side by side.

Walk on a flat first, then over easy bumps, until the action seems natural and the balance, with skis running together, comes easily. Until you're relaxed.

When you finally take up your poles—
use them!

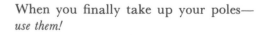

Reach out comfortably, plant the poles
firmly, lean out . . . and push.

Side Stepping

In side stepping, the feet are parallel, skis horizontal, body relaxed.

Step vigorously. Plant your edges forcefully.

In side stepping directly up the hill the poles are used mainly for balance.

In a traversing side step the lower hand is pushing hard, keeping the skier from slipping back.

Warm Up Maneuvers

Try these!

They are your introduction to the most important movements in skiing.

Give them no names yet. Let your body get used to the "feel" of these actions.

Try the snowplow on a well packed but not icy slope at first. Take an easy stance. Place your tips reasonably close together and force the heels of your skis apart. Don't let the skis ride flat or the outside edges will catch. Neither dig in the inside edges too much.

The Snowplow

The snowplow is the most elemental turn. Children invent it for themselves. But the snow-plow is more than just a valuable turn. It is an exercise in shifting the weight and controlling the edges.

1. Stand with knees bent comfortably and body relaxed.
2. Start straight down the hill in a wide snowplow position.
3. Shift the weight to one ski, and move your weight forward on this ski by adding to your ankle and knee-bend on that side.

4. Keep your inside shoulder and hip slightly advanced.
5. As you come around, shift your weight to the other ski; rotate your shoulders in the opposite direction.

As soon as you can, *lead into the turn with your inside shoulder* and arm. Next exaggerate this shoulder position and use it in every snowplow turn.

Leading the turn with the inside shoulder is a basic part of the modern turn.

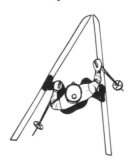

Modern Version   **Classical Stem Position**

The Kick Turn

Plant the rear pole firmly and in the position shown.

Kick up forcefully with the first ski lifted.

Bring the second ski around and place it close to the first and parallel with it.

Three common mistakes

1. Not standing horizontal. (Your skis go out from under you.)
2. Not kicking up forcefully. (You get hung up halfway around.)
3. Not turning far enough. (So one ski comes down across the other.)

Note the position of the poles. They are essential to keeping your balance.

The Sideslip

1. Stand with your skis horizontal, the upper edges holding.
2. Rock off your upper edges somewhat and feel your skis begin to slide sideways down the hill. Push with your upper pole if need be.
3. Control your slide. Keep your feet together and press knees together, skis parallel. Rock up your uphill edges to stop. Learn to control the speed of the sideslip by varying the bite of the edges.

When you can manage a sideslip directly down the fall line, make the skis work in other ways.

1. Lean forward, exerting more pressure on the tips. As they grip harder, the tails of the skis slip down and you begin a traversing sideslip backwards.
2. Then lean back, increasing the weight on the tails of your skis. You will go into a traversing sideslip forward.
3. Alternate, back and forth, making a wide S-shaped track in the snow.

The sideslip is the most important maneuver discussed in this chapter. From now on, you will need it every day you ski.

Tommy Corcoran, U.S.A., fourth in the 1960 Olymp

CHAPTER 2

The Modern Technique

"There are systems and theories of skiing"—so begins a well-known after-ski lyric: the Arlberg technique, the Allais school, the Swiss, the Canadian and many others. More recently, on the heels of modern racers, have come new universities of technique: the Official Austrian Method and the Modern French School. There are protagonists and antagonists, much sound and fury and tinkling symbol, to the delight of editors and the confusion of skiers. In spite of all the claims for this or that method, anyone watching the world's best skiers racing will observe that, wherever the men come from, they ski very much alike, and that individual differences based upon physical and psychological make-up are greater than the professed distinctions between the systems and theories of skiing.

Why then the diversity between schools? The explanation is simple. Skiing is still a dynamic sport, rapidly changing in both equipment and techniques. Taken separately the various schools seem quite different, but considered historically, as way stations along the path of a continuously evolving technique, they fall into logical sequence. Confusion comes because the epochs overlap: one may find methods that are basically Arlberg and Swiss of twenty-five years ago being taught side by side with modern reverse-shoulder techniques.

It would be wrong to suggest that one school completely displaces another. The survival of the snowplow turn and the abstem preparation for a downhill turn demonstrates that some of the techniques of ancient times are still valued controls today. On the other hand, it would be equally wrong to claim that there is nothing new in modern skiing.

Skiing is the product of skiers far more than of schools. Personalities and plain necessity have brought about most of the advances in technique. It was the necessity of high-speed alpine skiing on hard snow which developed the christiania and discarded the more elegant but less manageable telemark. Birger Ruud influenced a whole generation of jumpers, and among the alpine skiers Schneider, Durrance, Seelos, Allais, Eriksen, Sailer and many others have led a steady march toward modern controlled high-speed skiing.

You will need to know some new terms which describe certain distinct body movements. These you can see in the styles of modern skiers and you will come to feel them in your own skiing: *unweighting, rotation, angulation, festop*. Such technical-sounding words need not unnerve you. The actions they describe will be clear enough. A generation ago skiers had to struggle with worse jawbreakers: *vorlage, abstem, ruade,* etc. These words came over with the first wave of blond Teutonic instructors. There were patriotic outbursts against them at the time. Many a frustrated ski teacher, lacking English equivalents lumped the words together and threw them at his pupils in the universal form: "Benzeeknees." Skiing survived. It will survive these new terms. Call them the parts of speech, if you like, of the language of skiing.

The modern turn, the very basis of downhill skiing today, can be described in many ways, but before we consider the whole complex motion let us analyze its components:

Rotation   If a skier, suspended in air by a rope, turned his shoulders in one direction, his skis would automatically turn in the opposite direction. This is fundamental to the modern turn, the physics of the turn, sometimes called the "reverse shoulder." The twisting of the body proceeds upward and downward from the ankles and the degree of twisting above is followed by an opposite and equal twisting below.

This action cannot be demonstrated directly, standing on skis on the snow. The snow holds the skis locked fast. However, if you perch yourself on top of a small hard knoll so that your skis are free to swing, you can readily test this action and reaction. In actual skiing you free your skis by the process of:

Unweighting   That is, for an instant you relieve your skis from any downward

34

pressure of your body, then, rotating your upper body and hips one way you automatically turn your skis the other.

There are many ways to unweight your skis. As you travel over bumps, you can feel for an instant that giddy unaccustomed weightlessness. (Later on you will learn to use bumps in just this way, to initiate a turn.) You may unweight by actively jumping into the air, with the help of your poles, as one has to do in slush or breakable crust, and as Emile Allais of France, a pioneer in parallel skiing, did in his famous *ruade*. The jump method is effective and sometimes very useful, but it is rather beyond the co-ordination and confidence of most beginners.

A third method of unweighting is that of *suddenly dropping the hips*. This is not an unfamiliar action: have you ever stepped barefooted on a sharp stone? What happened? You dropped your hips at once, bending the knee and bringing the other foot hurriedly to the rescue. The action occurred without thinking. And that, in a general way, is what is meant by "unweighting" as it applies to the modern turn.

Rotation + unweighting = a turn? Not quite. We have not taken into account the centrifugal force of the skier's body in motion. That is to say, if you suddenly unweight your skis and rotate your body, turning your skis directly under your center of mass, you will be thrown downhill, falling to the outside of your turn. You must compensate for centrifugal force by letting your hips drop toward the inside of the turn, and by forcing your heels out, bracing them against the snow. This is called:

Angulation

The name comes from the rather sharp angle at the skier's waist. If the joints of the ankles, knees, and backbone were all universal joints, angulation would not be necessary and the body could assume a curved or bowed shape, a true "comma position." But they are not universal joints; they are hinges with a little extra play in them. Full rotation, a dropping of the hips, and a sharp angle at the waist are necessary to balance the centrifugal force of the skier. The sharper the turn the more sudden and complete is the dropping, rotation, and angulation.

In the pictures which follow, these three component parts of the modern turn are dissected for you in detail. Follow closely the separate actions of skis, feet, hips, shoulders, arms. You will learn the turn more easily if you can see the interplay of these components, both in the pictures and in your own actions.

The RISE-DROP exercises are specially designed to give you training in "unweighting." Practice them thoroughly on a variety of slopes until the *slow rise* and *quick drop* of the hips become familiar.

First it was "reverse shoulder," then it was "wedeln," then "mambo," the "comma position," and "heel thrust"—words thought to explain the modern technique in skiing. Like the blind man's description of an elephant, these words drew attention to certain aspects of the turn—the action of the shoulders, the thrust of the heels, the rhythm —but in so doing they may have obscured the total action. For example, it was thought that since Othmar Schneider "used the reverse shoulder," if you wanted to ski like Schneider, all you had to do was lead mightily with the inside shoulder. And thousands of skiers doggedly set their inside shoulders forward and wondered why their legs and skis still behaved in quite old-fashioned ways.

The fact is *Othmar did not "use" the reverse shoulder at all.* The turn he made was a beautifully integrated complex of actions involving his whole body and his skis; his inside shoulder did not initiate those actions; its leading position was the result of the total motion of his turn.

The so-called reverse shoulder is a good example of how ski techniques evolve. At first, style is pure motion, born out of skill and necessity. Then someone spots the action, or the end result of the action, and a name is invented. Then someone else conjures up a method of teaching and you have a new "school."

The reverse shoulder actually evolved quietly and naturally in many countries over a long period of time. In this country Dick Durrance, twenty years ago, was "ducking" his inside shoulder in order to get a few inches closer to the poles in slalom races. It worked; it was against the Arlberg tradition, but it worked. The great skiers of the postwar era—Eriksen, Sailer, Werner, Igaya—have all faced the problem of shaving off a hundredth of a second from each slalom turn. Of necessity they came up with similar answers: to get that much closer, they turned their backs completely to the poles. Then we began to hear of "reverse shoulders." But to accomplish this desired result, these skiers learned to let their weight drop to the inside, their heels thrust out, their edges biting in what we have come to call "the modern turn."

There are two major schools now teaching the modern turn: the Modern French School and the Austrian National School. They are quite different, not because the turn they teach is different but because the things they emphasize *in teaching* are different. The French School tends to emphasize *movements:* the movements of the hips, shoulders, feet, the twisting of the body, the dropping of the weight. The Austrian School tends to emphasize *positions:* the positions of the knees, heels, skis. Both methods produce excellent results.

We tend to favor the French school, not because their turns are better but because we like the concept that skiing is a motion, and because we believe that if skiers learn how to manage the large masses of the body—twisting the torso, dropping the hips—the lighter parts, arms, legs, feet will follow pretty well in their proper orbits.

Exercises and Uphill Turns

The many exercises presented in the pages of this chapter have only one purpose: to give you a step-by-step method of understanding and combining the various actions which make up a good downhill turn. From rise-drop exercises, running straight down a gentle slope, you proceed to unweighting on a traverse; then to unweighting followed by rotation; then to unweighting—rotation—and angulation. The turn will begin to take shape actually before you try to make it, for if these actions are emphatically carried out the turn must follow.

Your first turns will be uphill turns from a traverse, an extension or a modification of the sideslip which you learned in the first chapter and which every child discovers for himself. Learning will be easier if you can free yourself from complicating difficulties: speed, bumps, icy conditions, heavy snow, and the troublesome attentions of other skiers.

When you find that you can unweight your skis and turn uphill (in either direction) after running across a gentle traverse, the next step is simply to take more speed, a slightly steeper angle: run straight . . . slow rise . . . quick drop, rotate, angulate . . . knees together, feet together . . . swing uphill to a stop. By degrees the angle is steepened until you find that you are running straight down the fall-line and making turns in either direction.

What a long step ahead!

There is really only one more step to take: increasing the angle still further and turning downhill through the fall-line. The rest of downhill skiing is only a matter of learning the variations on this theme.

In all this discussion we have made no mention of arms and hands and poles. This is deliberate; no one learning to ski can think of more than one thing at a time or practice more than one action effectively. Pole handling and pole planting come next. If you can now link up a series of modern downhill turns, without using your poles, you are well on your way toward wedeln and actually deep into mambo already.

We are near the end of the business of this chapter: wedeln. Only three actions need to be learned: *planting the poles,* the sharp *heel thrust* ("festop" pronounced fess-top) that helps initiate a turn, and *unwinding* out of a rotated, angulated position.

Pole Handling

Ski poles at first seem clumsy extensions of the arms, designed for some misplaced arthropod. For the beginner, poles are useful mainly in keeping balance. For the racer, they mean a fast start and perhaps a fraction of a second gained on a flat or coming out of a slalom set. But the intermediate skier has a special use for his poles: planting the pole gives an exact point of reference for a turn; it is a declaration that now! after seconds of uncertainty, after hoping for a better patch of snow, now! the skis must turn.

Except in walking, climbing, and pushing with the poles, the arms should be carried in a relaxed position ahead. This is to say, in downhill running *you don't reach out and plant the pole and then let it drift back until your hand is behind you.* Instead you plant the pole firmly, let it travel back until the basket is about opposite your foot; then you extend your arm again and the pole comes free. Now let it swing forward like a pendulum held between thumb and forefinger.

First try planting the poles while running straight down a very gentle slope. Alternate the poles as you go. Then try it on a traverse and, holding the downhill pole to one side, out of the way, make a series of plantings of the uphill pole only. The point goes in near the tip of your uphill ski and comes out beside your uphill foot.

The
Uphill
Pole

The real test comes when you try to co-ordinate the action of hand and pole with what you already know: unweighting, rotation, angulation. This is not easy. The rhythm of hands and feet is likely to escape you. First try combining the planting of the uphill pole with the rise-drop exercise on a gentle traverse: from a crouch position you reach forward and plant the pole beside the tip of your uphill ski; as the pole rises to a vertical, you rise; as the point of the pole comes back to your feet, you suddenly drop your hips, extend your arm and let the pole swing forward to your tip again.

You need a simple rule to go by: *when the pole is low, you are low; when the pole is straight up, you are straight up.* And you need to remember that your forearms are always carried ahead.

When the rhythm of the poles harmonizes with the rhythm of rising and dropping, add the two other factors: rotation and angulation in an uphill turn. You will probably fall into two common errors at this point. First, you will be too timid about dropping, rotating, and angulating. Second, you will forget, while making a series of such turns on a long traverse, to unwind from your rotated position. The tendency will be, because you are concentrating on the poles, to leave your shoulders rotated downhill throughout the traverse, and this will spoil your chances for making a proper turn.

Each time you plant the uphill pole and make a brief turn around it, be sure you straighten up and unwind, squaring your shoulders again for the next turn.

The
Downhill
Pole

There is one more step to learn in mastering the action of the poles: how to plant the downhill pole in order to make a downhill turn. It is easier to eliminate the downhill turn at first and just concentrate on how to plant the pole. The rhythm is not the same as with the uphill pole. In this case you make a sudden *uphill* turn, angulating sharply and pushing down hard with your heels, and then, *just as you stop,* you reach out and plant the downhill pole at a convenient distance ahead.

Imagine yourself sliding up to a waiting bull and stopping just long enough to stab in one banderilla—that is the way to handle the downhill pole.

Next try several such abrupt stops in series on a gentle traverse, each time planting the downhill pole precisely as you stop. And lastly do the same series *not quite stopping,* letting your skis return to their former line before they stop, and squaring your shoulders at the conclusion of each brief "check." Again you will have consciously to remember to unwind. And you will have to remember not to leave the point of the pole in the snow so long that your skis slide into it.

38

Festop

The abrupt stop you have been making to plant the downhill pole has a name of its own: *Festop,* a fine French word which means literally "butt-stop." The word slides from between your lips and ends with a snap; it sounds the way the turn should look.

The festop is not a new action. For years skiers have known the trick of making a downhill turn with a quick uphill check to trigger it off. This is, in fact, another method of *unweighting,* for a sharp angulation downhill and a hard thrust of the heels can be used to flip the skier into his downhill turn. The Festop (pole planting included) is an emphatic declaration that now the turn must begin.

The Festop, followed at once with a downhill turn, should not be thought of as a separate action. It is part of that turn, and when done properly, it will feel that way. Rising and unwinding from the Festop position, the skier finds himself actually unweighting and rotating for the downhill turn. The end of one turn becomes the beginning of the next. . . . And that is *wedeln.*

If you have learned the Festop well, you have learned the rest, for wedeln is no more than a closely linked series of modern turns, each set off by a Festop finish of the turn above, each one using the recovery from one turn as the windup for the next. You will notice, watching other skiers, that in wedeln the skier's shoulders remain facing downhill while his skis move rapidly back and forth under him. The impression is a little like that of a whisk broom proceeding about its appointed duties straight down the fall-line.

The modern turn, of course, is not limited to such rapid changes of direction. There are really three kinds of turns: the short rhythmical wedeln which is the basis of slalom running; the medium arc turn suited to giant slalom; and the long radius turn, pulled out over bumps and jumps in one long sweep, which is the high-speed racing turn. Fundamentally they are the same. Unweighting, rotation, and angulation are present in each, but the longer the arc and the greater the speed the less visible are these three components.

So, too, is the recovery phase less apparent in the long radius turn. But it is there—the end of one turn serving as the beginning of the next.

Two great virtues of the modern turn should now be apparent: First, the fact that one turn leads naturally into the next without a break or sense of separation. Second, and just as important, is the fact that the recovery phase of the turn—when you are rising up again—gives you maximum grip with the edges just when you most need that grip.

In the longer turns the Festop type of initiation is not necessary, and unweighting may be no more of an action than simply riding off a bump . . . but all this is the subject of another chapter: the high-speed turn. For now be satisfied with good control, good rhythm—wedeln.

Rotation—The Basis of the Modern Turn

The skier stands on a hard knob of snow to demonstrate that rotation of the body in one direction automatically results in rotation of the skis in the opposite direction. This is exactly what happens in a modern turn: when you *unweight* your skis and *rotate* your body one way, your skis *turn* the other way. Rotation of the body is from the ankles up; you can feel it in your hips and shoulders, each twisting as far as they can.

The Rise-Drop Exercise

1. Rise from your running position.
2. Then drop quickly. (For an instant your skis are unweighted. They may even come entirely off the snow.)

Practice this first on a flat until the movement is familiar. Then do a series of rise-drop movements, running down a very gentle slope.

Rise slowly—drop quickly.

"To every action there is always an equal and contrary reaction."

NEWTON

Unweighting with Rotation

In skiing you "drop your hips" suddenly so that for an instant your skis are free from the grip of the snow. If at that instant you "rotate" your body one way, your skis will turn the other.

And if at the same time you thrust your heels out and make your edges bite (angulation) —you have a modern turn.

Unwinding, as you rise up again, your shoulders, hips, and skis automatically return to their initial position.

First study the arms and shoulders in the series—then the feet and skis. Then compare the two as they work together.

The position is called "angulation" because of the sharp angle formed at the waist. Angulation is necessary in order to compensate for the centrifugal force of turning. The sharper the turn the more acute the angle becomes.

Rotation, plus a sudden dropping of the hips, provides the outward thrust of the heels to make the turn—not vice versa!

Rotation, plus a sudden dropping of the hips, provides the outward thrust of the heels to make the turn—not vice versa

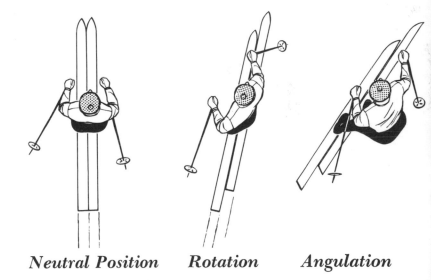

Neutral Position   *Rotation*   *Angulation*

Unweighting on a Gentle Slope or on a Traverse

How does one learn the modern turn? By learning one thing at a time.

The following pages show a progression of maneuvers which, when followed, will lead you to wedeln.

On a gentle slope, practice a slow rising movement, followed by a sudden dropping toward the skis. Keep your arms to the side, relaxed; poles pointed back and out of the way and uphill ski slightly advanced.

Unweighting and Rotation

Your first turn! Try a series of unweighting movements on a traverse. Then, without stopping, just as you are dropping and unweighting your skis, rotate your upper body so that you face down the hill. Do not worry what your skis will do, think about your upper body.

The uphill arm and shoulder are thrust ahead—far ahead—as the skier sinks into the turn. Note that the skier's upper body leans down the hill while his hips swing toward the slope. This is angulation.

Series: Unweighting

ition

The skier starts to rise: having brought his shoulders back to the normal running position, his skis return to their former "line," traversing down the hill. He is now ready to drop into the angulated position and turn again.

Poles are held to the side out of the way, where they can be forgotten for the time being.

Turning Out of the Fall Line
Without Planting the Poles

After mastering turning uphill on a slight traverse, steepen your angle downhill and turn again. Finally you can go straight down. The turn is not different because of this. Go through the same movements— unweighting, rotation, and angulation—as before.

Do not try this on a steep hill, or one full of struggling bunnies. Pick a slope where you can take your time, do one thing at a time, and relax.

When you can make smooth, confident turns in each direction . . . it is time to put them in a sequence.

Again on a gentle slope and in good snow conditions.

Unweighting—Rotation—Angulation

Hold your poles to the side and forget them. Think of unweighting, rotation, and angulation combined into one synchronous motion—and the motion repeated from one side to the other.

Common Mistakes:
1. Not dropping fast enough.
2. Leaning into the hill, carrying the weight on the inside ski. This tends to throw you over backward.
3. Letting your skis drift apart. (Can you hold a dollar bill between your knees?)
4. Being too stiff and tense.

This is an act of composition. Choose smooth snow conditions and a hill that is neither too slow nor too steep.
By forgetting your poles you can concentrate on the feel of correct body movements.

Traversing—Planting Only the Uphill Pole Without Turning

Choose a gentle slope and *ski it slowly*. Keep both hands well in front—not out to the side and never behind you. Your arms are relaxed, partly bent, and your wrists flexible. As you reach out to plant one pole, you crouch—in goes the pole near the tip of your ski. As the pole rises straight up, you rise straight up—as the pole drops again, you crouch.

Remember your hand does not travel back, beside or behind you. And you keep your shoulders square with your path at all times.

Common Mistakes:
1. Skiing too fast.
2. Not crouching deep enough prior to planting the pole.
3. Stiff wrist, tight grip.
4. Twisting the shoulders.

Now plant the pole and as you go by it drop, rotate and angulate. Your skis will turn uphill.

Planting the Downhill Pole
During an Uphill Stop

Running on a traverse, stand high on your skis, then drop and make an uphill turn. *Just as you come to a stop* plant your downhill pole at an easy arm's length ahead. This is the Festop.

Your uphill arm and pole are carried in a comfortable position out of the way, and forgotten.

Common Mistakes:
1. Not angulating enough. You should lean over your skis.
2. Planting the pole too soon or too late. Jab it in hard just as you stop.

The Festop (fess-top!)

This time you don't quite stop. As you make your swing and plant your downhill pole, rise up, unwind, let the pole drift out of the snow and your skis continue the traverse.

Thus you can do a series of checks, timed with planting the downhill pole.

Timing is the essence of co-ordination. Until the poles, body, and skis are felt to be working in complete harmony you may be sure your timing is off.

In a sideslip you let the skis drift obliquely downhill. In a Festop the tips do not shift from the traversing line, but the heels make a quick arc downhill. You angulate sharply and the heels are thrust down hard—for only a split second, enough to trigger your swing. The Festop should be learned well for wedeln is a series of closely linked Festops.

On a smooth traverse:

1. Do a single sharp Festop, making your edges bite hard and planting the poles just as you stop.
2. Do a series of sharp Festops, but do not quite lose forward motion in between.
3. Then end with a Festop leading into a downhill turn.

Note how the downhill pole is planted, while the uphill arm is relaxed and carried ahead. Note, too, the full angulation as the skier makes his Festop.

The Modern Turn

A Festop followed by unweighting, rotation, angulation.
That is a Festop leading into a modern downhill turn.
Note: hands, poles, hips, knees, edges.

Wedeln

A series of modern turns

Theme in Variations

Learning to ski is like starting up a narrow gully at the bottom of a mountain. You don't know where the gully leads and you aren't even sure why you've started. But you have started. It is easier to keep climbing than go down, and something tells you it looks more interesting. You learn as you go, the gully broadens, you begin to see new snow fields ahead and in the distance the higher mountains push into view. You have the fever; each step, a reward in itself, urges you on with growing exhilaration.

And finally you arrive—an able and confident skier at last—not at the top, but in a great basin near the top where you can spend the best days of your life skiing. Suddenly it hits you: this is why you learned, plodding through the clumsy first stages, through the complexities of technique, not even knowing why when you started. Around you are still the peaks—racing, touring, ski mountaineering, the sciences and professions concerned with mountain or arctic research, and the variety of pleasures open to expert skiers. These summits, unimagined earlier, are yours for the taking. The climb has been worth it.

This chapter—and the skiing itself—should set you free, able to handle with zest any reasonable slope or snow condition. Some of the things discussed in this chapter are clearly tricks and stunts done for the sheer joy of skiing; others are the special techniques necessary for special snow conditions. Perhaps the distinction is not worth making. For example: is *skating* a stunt or a technique? There are times when a long gentle slope, lying luxuriously in unbroken snow, asks nothing so much as to be taken in long swinging, skating strokes; and there are times, shooting a flat in a slalom race or blasting out of a tight set of gates, when three hard skating steps can mean the margin of victory.

Skating is not shown in sequence pictures here, for anyone can learn for himself the technique of rocking from one ski to the other in a leisurely rhythm. As with bicycle riding, the faster you go the easier it is to balance. A nice test of your balance and edge control is ending your skating strokes with a turn on one ski, as a skater would, either on an "inside edge" or an "outside edge."

A cousin of skating is *wedeln on your outside ski*. It will be valuable largely as an exercise in controlling your weight by a subtle blend of rotation and edge rocking. The action especially good for one who tends to sit back and ride his inside ski.

A variant of the Festop type of wedeln is the *abstem wedeln,* or snowplowing briefly with the downhill ski before going into a downhill turn. Like the Festop it is an action sharp and to the point, throwing you at once into an unweighted position from which to make your turn. Being a very natural maneuver, the abstem is by no means new; it was already ancient when tied together with the rotation and counter-rotation of the arms which was sacred doctrine twenty-five years ago. The abstem start of a turn is versatile; it is perfectly suited to the modern downhill turn, being essentially a half Festop.

Strictly in the category of stunts are the horizontal 360° turn, the somersault, and the layout somersault. All of them require a sharp up-shoot take-off (or looping take-off) to give the skier sufficient height and time to perform these astonishing tricks. Such maneuvers should not be treated frivolously. Only an expert, with tumbling and diving experience, should attempt them; there are no halfway exits from a somersault.

Mambo   Mambo is an ear-catching word, and eye-catching rhythm (and an edge-catching maneuver if your technique is not equal to your temptations). Mambo is a ballroom exhibition, the ballroom being a gentle slope properly dusted with powder and peopled with young

58

things. There the skier oozes down the fall-line and by the rotation of his upper body and the rocking of his ankles insinuates his series of partial turns among the stembogens and scrape-christies of the multitude. There is no sliding on the turns, only a succession of curves guided by the bend of the skis and carved by sharp edges. If there were snow snakes—other than the after-ski variety—mambo is what they would do.

All skiers must be able to handle bumps. The expert skier however *uses* them deliberately: for jumps and turns and gaining speed. He derives his greatest pleasure from accepting the challenge that bumps offer him. Among the jumps you will learn to do and delight in are the *pre-jumps* used on the large rolling bumps and pitches where to fly off the crest of the bump would throw you beyond any feasible landing. This subject is treated in detail in the chapter on Downhill. Other soaring jumps are those connected with running off cornices or other roof-like edges that lead out over a steep landing. *Cornice jumping* and the *geländesprung* give the downhill runner the sensation of hovering for a moment, weightless in space. Speed is not necessary. Indeed, your first jumps should be made with only enough speed to clear the selected obstruction. With a cornice jump you simply approach the edge in a crouch and at a reasonable speed, plant your poles firmly near the lip, spring, push down hard on your poles, and then *lift your feet up and relax.* Nice judgment is required in rolling your weight forward far enough so your body and skis follow the slope under you.

Bumps

In coming down, you stretch your legs down to meet the snow and take up the shock of landing with ankles, knees, and hips.

Moguls offer even more complicated problems, for moguls are usually multiple and are rarely avoidable. These sharp bumps, like man-made cataracts, are found on any heavily skied steep slope. To the beginner they are a horror. He must scrape and scramble through somehow in order to gain the smoother slope beyond. But the good skier, capable of running such white water, finds that moguls provide an exciting, rapid-fire test of his ability to combine pre-jumping, wedeln, and riding the air in a gelandi. He finds that there are sequences of bumps where the easiest and best way to pass is to ride up off of one bump, clear one or two in between, and land on the downslope of yet another.

The *Geländesprung* is not as difficult as it seems. Speed is not essential, nor is a large bump necessary. For your first experiments, pick a small bump with a sharp upshoot and a reasonably good landing beyond. Place your hands firmly on the tops of your poles and plan to set the poles in the snow near the top of the bump. As you make your approach, be sure your knees and ankles are well bent. Then, as your skis are bridging the curve to the crest, you plant your poles (like two banderillas, this time), spring up, push down hard on your poles, pick up your feet . . . and float.

Pole
Jumps

On the average ski slope your choice of "lines" may be wide enough to let you circumnavigate any hazardous stretch. But many times in your skiing life you will have to face tough conditions and get down. The glare ice of a freeze-up, after a rain or thaw, presents one such unavoidable difficulty; with sharp edges and a determination to make them bite, you can run ice without difficulty. For the beginner deep moist new powder (mashed potatoes) is perhaps the greatest hazard, owing to the danger of being spread-eagled in a forward fall.

Other types of snow condition which can be utterly exhausting are slush or breakable crust. While they are quite different in nature, their effect on the skier is similar. They both tend to lock the skis in awkward positions, to stick unexpectedly, to throw the skier off balance forward. The method of skiing both slush and breakable crust is the same: you have to free your skis entirely from the grip of the snow in order to make your turn. The ordinary method of unweighting is not sufficient. You have actively to jump, rotating, angulating and completing the first part of the turn while still in the air. For this, the pole jump, using both poles (if you are going slow) or just the downhill pole (if you are going fast), is the most effective technique. Kick-pole jumps can be used to reverse direction if you are scarcely moving at all; it is simply a kick turn completed all in one jump.

We have mentioned most of the nightmarish snow conditions skiers will get themselves into. It is time to speak of one where all the dreams come true:

Deep
Powder

Button your collar, pull up your hood, attack deep powder head on. Pick a slope steeper than you dare. Ski faster than you think you can. If you submerge, you submerge—a quick dip is refreshing. Soon you will find you are making long smoking arcs on a trackless mountain, riding a cushion of crystals and air that surge around you, drifting into a knee-deep scoop of a turn and wanting to burst your lungs with a shout—this is play for an artist in a magic medium.

The technique of turning is not different: unweighting, rotation, angulation serve you here as on a hard-packed slope. There are a few necessary modifications, however:

1. On hard-packed snow you had to weight your outside ski to make the edges bite. In powder the whole ski is your edge. In deep snow you must weight both skis about equally or one will plunge and the other will climb.

2. In powder you have to sit back somewhat so your skis can plane up.

3. In powder you should use limber skis. Stiff racing skis tend to plunge.

If you fall you may find yourself head down in bottomless fluff. The snow will seek out and invade every ungarded chink. So be it. Roll rapidly over—as a cat in air—and place your feet below you. If it is impossible to get a purchase on the stuff you're stuck in, take off your poles and, holding them crossed in front of you, push yourself out to a more manageable stance.

In deep powder, you need sonar in your feet. Your skis must ride together in three dimensions. Especially in turns you must hold knees and skis together, for if one ski wanders, it may wind up back of your neck. Yet this is not as difficult a technique as it sounds, if you take sufficient speed, sit back a little and weight the skis more or less evenly.

One word of warning: powder snow and steep slopes are a formula for *avalanches*. Many a skier has let deep powder tempt him to his last ride down. While the subject of avalanches deserves expert treatment beyond the scope of this book, some of the principles for anticipating danger are mentioned in the chapter on Touring.

This chapter, the previous one, and the chapter on Downhill Skiing are probably the most important in the book. Most skiers will spend their lives among the things of these pages; he who has mastered the modern turn and all its variations would be recognized as an expert skier anywhere in the world.

Kick—Jump—Turn

Take very little speed. Hands on top of poles. Plant the poles firmly, jump up with the uphill foot and kick hard with the downhill foot. Lean back, throwing your tips as high as possible. Then twist downhill and bring your skis together under you.

Now try both feet together as Stein Eriksen does.

The "butterfly" turn—a good exhibition of edge control by Hans Nogler of Sun Valley.

The Mambo

In simplest terms: mambo is wedeln without Festops and without the use of poles. Therefore, mambo must flow from rotation—exaggerated rotation. Actually mambo is a very subtle, soft-spoken interchange between rotation of the body above and rocking of the ankles below.

1. Start as you would for wedeln, traversing down a smooth slope.
2. Start your first small turn with a Festop, or go directly into mambo by over-rotating your upper body toward the bottom of the hill. Let your downhill hand trail behind you and your uphill hand come clear across in front.
3. Flatten your skis; as you unwind, they will turn downhill . . . as your skis come around, rock up on your edges and again over-rotate . . . flatten your skis, unwind . . . etc.

Unwinding from one turn becomes the initiation of the next, but unlike the versatile wedeln, mambo can only be done where conditions favor the full development of a sequence based upon over-rotation.

64

Geländesprung

Christian Pravda of Austria at the top of his flight in a
geländesprung. Four factors have combined to give him his
height: the speed with which he rode over the mogul; his
jump; the spring in his skis; and the force of his push on the
top of his poles.

Knowing what he is doing, Pravda is completely at ease. He
may clear intervening bumps and land on the far side of a
chosen mogul, or he may begin a turn in the air and complete
it after he lands.

Wedeln on the Outside Ski

This is good practice if you constantly find yourself "back and on your inside ski."

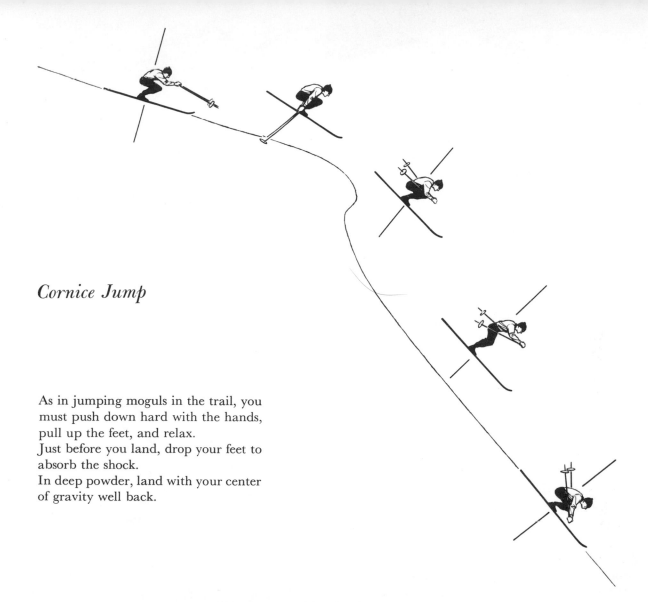

Cornice Jump

As in jumping moguls in the trail, you
must push down hard with the hands,
pull up the feet, and relax.
Just before you land, drop your feet to
absorb the shock.
In deep powder, land with your center
of gravity well back.

Ernie McCullock

Abstem Wedeln

Abstem means literally to "stem down" or "away from"—that is, a stem with your downhill ski. Call it half a Festop if you like. Try it first at slow speeds and work for smoothness.

Make the half stem quickly and with sharp edging so that, when you release the pressure, your ski snaps back into the parallel position, tossing you into your turn.

Crouch Mambo

Here is a wonderful way to find rhythm: Take good speed and start in a crouch while traversing. Abstem with the lower ski and swing the upper body toward the bottom of the slope. When you have twisted to your maximum, flatten your skis and swing back; your skis will then turn in the opposite direction.

Tumbling

A sixty-foot swan dive somersault by the world's master, Stein Eriksen of Norway.

This is tumbling on skis and you should know tumbling or diving before trying it.

The jump should be three feet high with an upshoot of 45°.

It should be followed by a flat section of thirty to forty feet long then a gentle slope for landing.

The commonest mistakes are:

1. Not building the jump with enough upshoot.
2. Not taking enough speed.
3. Not tucking the head down forcefully after leaving the lip.
4. Staying in a tuck too long (doing one and one-half somersaults).

Deep Powder

"Pick a slope steeper than you dare. Ski faster than you think you can."

HANS STEINER, ST. MORITZ

CHAPTER 4

Touring
Ski Mountaineering
Touring Equipment
Avalanches

Touring

Cross-country skiing is not just for the racer, or the occasional hardy misanthrope of Scandinavian extraction. It is a sport so broad as to escape definition, one which probably opens the door for more people to a wider variety of pleasures than any other phase of skiing. The youngster of six who takes his skis and poles and goes off "sploring" on the hills is following the trail of Amundsen and Nansen. The ski mountaineer with his camp on his back, who works an expedition into the heart of a range of mountains, needs cross-country techniques to get him there, but no more so than the middle-aged novice who wants only a gentle hike on skis. The elder skier of seventy-five, sliding through the templed twilight of red fir or pine or sequoia, cherishes his partnership with skis and pack since they sustain him in those adventures still open to him in winter.

One could go further and say that cross-country skiing is the primordial sport itself, as old as man moving across snow for whatever purpose: food, shelter, trade, talk, war, love. It is to cross-country skiing that all Scandinavian peoples turn when they seek recreation in winter.

It was cross-country skiing, too, which preserved Finland during its winter war of 1939 and made such wreckage of the invader, forty times larger.

Yet for all its broad possibilities, cross-country skiing (touring) is almost unknown in this country except as it is mistakenly identified with racing. Cross-country racing is a wholly different matter (and the subject of another chapter in this book). The carry-over from one to the other, however, is considerable. Like learning to swim, the value of cross-country racing is in the lifelong freedom it gives—the techniques of moving easily, rapidly, efficiently, uphill and down, the knowledge of suitable waxes and equipment, the love of going it quietly with hills and friends of your own choosing.

Most people think of touring as something to do in the Alps, or in the Jotunheim of Norway, where chains of cabins are maintained especially for winter's finest blessing: spring skiing in the high mountains. We have one such cabin chain here in America, too, built by the Sierra Club of California and running the Sierra crest between Donner and Echo Summits. And there are a scattering of individual cabins in some of our best ski country. But touring is not something far away, exclusive or expensive. It is wherever snow falls. For many it lies just beyond the doorstep, or at least as close as the nearest ski area. New Hampshire has its woods roads and trails, its outing-club cabins, and its incomparable Mt. Washington. Vermont has its sky-parlor pastures. New York and the northern Midwestern states have broad farmland and open hilly woods, while the Rocky Mountain states, the Northwest, and California have been more prodigally endowed with ski terrain than ever they were with copper, silver, or gold.

What has been missing is any knowledge of how to go. Equating skiing with mechanical entertainment, and evaluating the sport entirely by what it costs, is now the basis of our ski culture. The rest is largely forgotten. Equipment, too, has played a large part in making skiing a downhill addiction. The stiff boots, heavy skis, and nailed-down bindings make walking a painful, ungainly process. . . .

But have you ever tried touring skis? Have you ever tried taking your family out on a winter picnic? Leaving the bucket chairs and clanking devices for sunny hills in untouched snow? Making a climb and a cook-out and an exploration of it?

Touring Equipment

Touring gear is light and inexpensive. A fair start can be made with no more than a set of cable lugs placed forward under the toe plates of ordinary bindings. Touring is only walking up and running down on skis; flexible boots, loose bindings, and climbing wax are the only variations from normal equipment. (For those who find they like touring,

detailed information about skis, wax, and running techniques are to be found in the later sections of this book.)

Common sense would add a few more items of equipment, even for a one-day trip, for people get lost and snowstorms overtake the best-laid schemes:

A pack	Ace bandage and stout cord
Extra clothing and parka	Paper or candle for starting fire
Matches	An aluminum ski tip
Ski waxes	Extra binding and straps
Map and compass	Emergency food
Knife	Sunburn preventive & sunglasses

Ski Mountaineering

The business of ski mountaineering—taking an exploring party into the high mountains in winter—though a form of touring, is far removed from casual snow picnicking. As with any such expedition, great competence and careful planning is required: it is not a subject for offhand treatment here and the interested reader would be well advised to consult some standard text such as the *Manual of Ski Mountaineering*, published by the Sierra Club of California.

Avalanches

The same is true of this vast subject. We would not attempt to write less than a book on avalanches were we not certain that there have been, are, and always will be, skiers killed because they failed to consult either the proper books or their common sense before venturing into the mountains.

Avalanches are one of the stark forces of the earth, to be rated—in human affairs at least—with floods, earthquakes, and hurricanes. Let us be clear on two points: first, if you are caught in an avalanche, it is mostly luck if you survive; second, the best way to avoid such a disaster is not to tempt one.

It would be wrong to imply that most ski slopes are avalanche chutes trembling to let go. They are not. Avalanches are alpine phenomena. But it would be equally wrong, in a chapter on touring, to suggest that the possibility of avalanches is negligible. Mt. Washington, Sun Valley, Aspen, Alta, and even the mild Mt. Ralston in a domesticated section of the Sierra have shaken down devastating snow slides, and will again when the conditions are ripe.

Avalanches are tricky and unpredictable—that is the first thing to know about them. Steep slopes, heavy snow (dry, wet, or wind-crusted), and variable conditions of weather and temperature will always breed avalanches. But beyond these common circumstances, under optimum conditions, a wind-slab avalanche can break loose on

76

HELMY BROMBERGER

DAVID BROWER

a slope no steeper than 30°. As would be expected, snow slides tend to form over and over in the same places, under steep ridges and cornices. Snow fields and couloirs which annually clean out the young trees should provide warning enough to the observant skier. And yet in some of our more alpine resorts, as in Europe, disastrous slides *can* occur on well-skied slopes and bowls.

A factor common to most avalanches is the presence of a deep layer which is hard and distinct and unbonded to the mass of snow above. Rain unmixed with snow, or a sun-baked glassy surface, or sleet and hail, or simply the "rotting out" of snow underneath a thick wind crust may provide the separation and sliding surface that makes a snow field unstable. An avalanche after a heavy snow in April may come down because of a soaking rain in early January, which was followed by clear freezing weather. Or it may come down on the ball bearings of a hail storm two months earlier. Or it may come down because wind built up a heavy crust over the top of deep, loose, powdery snow.

Local knowledge of the common avalanche chutes must therefore be supplemented with information both as to recent snowfalls and as to unusual icing or sunny conditions throughout the winter. Sometimes the skier may discover for himself the presence of danger by plunging his ski pole upside down into the snow. If loose snow, or wind pack over loose snow, can be felt distinctly different from a deep solid crust, it is wise to assume that the avalanche danger is very real.

There are three kinds of conditions likely to produce avalanches: 1. *Deep Powder Snow:* Powder snow requires a fairly steep slope to slide. Such avalanches tend to form on the *sheltered side* of ridges, under the cornices, where the heaviest accumulations of snow are dumped. Thus a mountain of light snow may be balanced there, crystal on top of crystal, ready for the slightest jar to set it loose. The slide tends to form at the top, gathering mass and momentum as it goes. It strikes swiftly, and it moves almost without a sound at first; later, falling with almost gravitational acceleration, it fumes toward the valley floor carrying tons of air and crystals in a mass and forming a devastating shock wave or avalanche wind.

Powder-snow avalanches are as apt to kill through inhalation (drowning the victim with ice crystals) as by the crushing weight of snow. Fortunately most powder-snow slides follow traditional chutes and come down during the first day following a heavy storm.
2. *Wind-Slab:* Wind-slab is a heavily compacted layer of snow, often quite thick, formed by wind blowing over a relatively stable layer of deep powder. It is not the same thing as the wind-plastered snow that forms on open mountainsides that are constantly subjected to wind, but a special situation where the thick crust lies over a mass of loose snow.

Its presence unsuspected, it may let go in an area normally safe and surprisingly gentle. Moreover the danger exists long after the warning of a heavy fall of snow is forgotten.

Wind-slab usually gives fair warning: there is a hollow sound underfoot like that made by tunking a ripe pumpkin; or there is the thump of snow settling as you walk on it; or the sharp sound of cracking. The cracks themselves, sometimes very small, can often be seen shivering out ahead of your skis. And the presence of a loose hollow base may be ascertained by probing with the ski pole. That is the time to turn back, for when wind-slab lets go, the whole slope shatters and comes down in the same instant, like a deluge of cement blocks.

3. *Wet Snow:* Wet-snow avalanches are formed when snow has been deeply saturated with water (from warm rains or hot weather) and then, by cooling and drying, has lost its stability. Typically these are the mid-afternoon or late-afternoon slides. They may start with no more impetus than the sliding of snow from under your skis. They move slowly, but once started they tend to dig deeper and deeper until in the end they may gouge out the field down to the rocks. Heavy with tons of water, wet-snow avalanches have enormous destructive capacities, and when they finally squeeze to a stop, the whole avalanche mass freezes tight.

What to do if caught in an avalanche? The matter is often entirely beyond your control. If you are in the path of an avalanche, or if you are actually in it, you will try to ski out to the side. With wet-snow avalanches you have a pretty fair chance of success. In powder snow and wind-slab, where escape is next to hopeless, you try to release your

MILOV STEINER, ZÜRICH

skis and, by swimming, keep on the surface. In a powder-snow avalanche, if you can master panic, you may remember about not breathing in the powder-filled air . . . but all in all, there is no phase of skiing where refusal to take any chances whatever has so few drawbacks.

There are certain standard rules for keeping out of avalanche trouble:

1. When in doubt don't try it—that is the first and last and best rule. Unless the terrain is certain, let a new heavy fall of snow settle for a day before going touring. Under no conditions accept the risk of inclined wind-slab.
2. In an unfamiliar alpine area, inquire of some qualified native as to the common avalanche patterns, any recent heavy snowfall, and any peculiar icing conditions occurring during the winter.
3. When climbing, stick to the big timber, the tops of ridges, and keep away from cornices.
4. When the necessities of the tour absolutely force you to consider a potentially dangerous slope, first test the snow under you and examine other ridges and couloirs for evidence of slides.
5. If you have to venture on a possible avalanche slope, be conscious, always, of where your best escape route lies.
6. Under such circumstances a ski party must spread out. Roping up would be madness. One hundred fifty feet between members of a party is a minimum, and each member should be trailing a length of colored string from his waist. With luck some part of this telltale string may be found on the surface after the avalanche has stopped and so lead to a buried skier.
7. If you have to climb, climb straight up. If you have to traverse, climb straight up first and then traverse at the top.

These few hints about avalanches by no means cover the subject. And it would be wrong to leave the impression that cross-country skiing is likely to be dangerous. It can be—by deliberate choice—but in general cross-country skiing is the least dangerous, most peaceful, and inexpensive form of the sport.

T. WEIR, GLASGOW

Downhill Skiing

Downhill running dominates modern skiing in all areas except Scandinavia. It is no wonder that this is true: downhill skiing provides the most speed, variety, and sustained excitement, the largest crowds, the highest cost, and greatest hazards of all phases of the sport. Young and old enjoy it, years before and decades after they have any thought of racing. Children who are sternly forbidden a candy bar during the week soon learn that on Sundays the parents can be shaken down for five-dollar all-day ski-lift tickets and hot dogs and chocolate galore. For many reasons, biological as well as gravitational, most skiers will be downhill runners all their lives. This chapter, therefore, is the culmination of all that deals with general skiing and a natural transition into racing. Certain refinements of technique are all that remain to be considered: those related to the wind pressure of high-speed skiing (the various crouches, and per contra, wind-checking), and those necessitated by fast going over bumpy terrain (checking, jumping, pre-jumping, running multiple bumps, etc.).

Wind   At slow speeds, *e.g.,* for general recreational skiing and slalom racing, the drag of the wind is inconsequential. But at speeds of 30 m.p.h. or more, wind pressure begins to be a factor, and under racing conditions the resistance of the air becomes a matter at least as important as the terrain itself. A skier traveling in a low crouch at 60 to 70 m.p.h. can, by simply standing up straight, reduce his speed nearly a third. This is called *wind-checking;* it is a device commonly resorted to by downhill racers and downhill skiers when they feel they are approaching a difficult stretch too fast.

There are, of course, many degrees of wind-checking, ranging from a medium crouch to a full-height stand with the arms held out, or fist on hips and elbows out to the side. In the same way there are several kinds of crouches, which vary with the terrain, the need for rest, the strength of the skier, etc.

There are bound to be some who, reading this, will protest: "But why should anyone want to ski fast? It is difficult enough to ski slow." The question will have to be referred to other authority: skiers will always go as fast as their skill will permit—and a little bit faster.

Bumps   Bumps, sharp-crested humps, long rolling knolls, steep pitches with flat outruns, multiple bumps (moguls), and similar terrain features, which present abrupt changes in direction, are the constant proving grounds for downhill skiers and the standard tests in any good downhill race. How such obstacles are to be ridden depends largely on the speed, the shape of the obstruction, and what lies below. Some bumps you can take simply by running straight over them in a semi-crouched position and letting your legs work like pistons, so that the main weight of the body continues in an undisturbed line. Some bumps can be ridden entirely—take-off, flight, and landing—in a crouch position. Others, too sharp to ride over, you can avoid by suddenly hoisting your knees and feet, so that your skis skim over the crest of the bump.

Another group of bumps, or sharp declivities, "waterfalls" etc., with steep drops and flat outruns, cannot be negotiated simply by flying off in a crouch. Long jumps are involved and you may completely overjump the landing, piling up on the flat below. A skier once in the air can do very little to modify his trajectory. Whatever his forward speed, he can only drop 16 feet in the first second, 64 feet in two seconds. If his forward speed is too great, he can carry beyond any reasonable landing surface.

Large jumps of this kind present a nice test of judgment: how fast to go, whether to wind-check or edge-check above, where to make the jump, how far to let the body weight roll forward in order to be in balance on landing.

For such large problems the *pre-jump* was invented, a method of jumping early, lifting the legs to clear the crest of the bump, and

84

landing on the desired steep slope beyond. Perfect timing is essential, for to jump too soon or too gently means that the skier will ricochet off the crest; to jump too late will only increase the length of the jump.

The expert downhill runner no less than the intermediate skier or the child, must always be in control—thinking ahead, planning his course and speed to suit the terrain below, and, where necessary, wind-checking or edge-checking. The nature of his control may not be readily apparent. He is not slamming his skis into a skid; he is not approaching each bump with a hesitant stem. Instead, he will be pulling his turn out over a hundred yards of flying snow, but his weight is on his edges and his edges are at work, their action equally stretched out. He may not show a snowplow, but in running straight over a mess of bumps his tips will often be canted slightly together and the outside edges slightly raised so they will not catch on a bump and send him cartwheeling. He will not be doing practice-slope Festops, but you will see his skis slashing into an uphill turn before he rounds off into a long downhill turn or lines into a pre-jump pitch.

These maneuvers are identical with those of the preceding chapters. The fact that an expert can perform them nonchalantly at high speeds means only that he has done them thousands of times at slower speeds.

Sometimes a check or an attempted turn is just the wrong thing to do: when things suddenly get out of control in rough bumps, when a patch of ice has set you back on your heels for a critical instant, or a wandering stembogen pedestrian has turned, or failed to turn, or fallen directly in front of you—then it may be that the only thing to do is put your skis together and bull it through over bumps and jumps until you gain an easier turning slope beyond.

That is downhill: it produces accidents—and addicts.

Checking

Downhill Racing

Strange to say downhill racing was not the invention of the Austrians or the Swiss or the Germans, or even the wild men who founded the Downhill Only Club of Great Britain. The Arlberg-Kandahar race, most famous of all downhill events, was begun in 1928, a joint effort of the British and Austrians. The first international championship in downhill (Fédération Internationale de Ski) was held at Mürren, Switzerland, in 1931, while downhill-slalom races were not given formal Olympic status until 1936. The famous people associated with these early European races—Prager, Fuhrer, Matt, Seelos, Allais, and many others were all Johnny-come-latelies, three quarters of a century behind the real pioneers of downhill racing.

These, the noble ancestors of our sport, were about as unlikely a crew in about as implausible an area as anyone can imagine. They were sour-dough miners, wintering it out in the gold diggings of the Feather River Valley in California. They had no stretch pants. They had no hundred-dollar multilaminated Austrian skis with Kofix bases. Instead they planed out their homemade twelve-foot planks, fitted them with toe straps, smeared them with very secret dope, and went out to race unshaven and full of amateur spirits. The hill was a mountainside just out of town and the course was simple: a straight shot through scrub pine to the valley floor. Simultaneous starts were always used, and the finish was in a bar where money prizes and libations were dispensed.

The first of these winter carnivals was in 1857. Such festivities were repeated yearly until the rush for gold subsided and the towns reverted into sand. Good records of the contests were kept and the records show that speeds of over 60 m.p.h. were not uncommon.

Such were our sporty forefathers . . . those who would prefer more standard family portraits—"gentlemen rankers," forsooth—to place over the mantel of their minds, must come down to 1933 when the first National Downhill Championship was held on the old carriage road on Mt Moosilauke. The race was won by Bem Woods, a jumper (just as Birger Ruud won the first Olympic Downhill, in Garmisch)—but then those were the days of all-round skiers, loose bindings, the Arlberg crouch, when trails were a pipeline of spruce and the best turn was a controlled fall.

Of all ski races, downhill is the toughest. The same exactness and memory work that is required in slalom is demanded in downhill but extended over two miles or more of bumpy terrain. The same daring "to lean out on your luck" that the jumper has to have is put to the test here, too, but stretched out over several minutes of intense effort and at speeds ranging from 50 to 70 m.p.h. No other race compares to downhill in danger, real or imagined, and probably no other race asks so much of the skier.

Yet downhill is not, as many suppose, a race only for those having Neanderthal strength and no brains above their flattened eyeballs. It is a skilled performance planned to the inch from top to bottom, studied, rehearsed, and carried out. Cool judgment at high speeds, acrobatic control, confidence, the ability to relax under enormous physical and mental pressure are at a premium in a downhill race. The dangers are obvious. In some cases the skiers are asked to play their luck too hard. But the solutions too are apparent: trails cut wide enough, snow packed hard and wide, control gates set when necessary. (See Appendix: Alpine Ski Races.)

Racing is not the ultimate purpose of skiing or of this book, but it is one of the great choices given to those who have learned to ski well. And there is more to racing than just clocking a fast time. Racing puts to the test all that a man has in the way of technique, courage, stamina, good judgment. It sharpens the wits of the racer and cements forever the union of the man and his skis. But the value of racing cannot be described in words. It is part of the "feel" of skiing mentioned at the beginning. One who has not raced will never quite understand, and one who has raced needs no explanations.

Training for downhill racing consists largely of accustoming your mind and body to the feel of speed. It is a matter of confidence at least as much as of technique, and it goes without laborious saying, therefore, that you cannot ski *fast* until you can ski *well*.

The time for thinking about technique is past; technique must be a part of you, automatically responding to what the eye and mind say are the terrain problems immediately ahead. If you are still worried about "how good you look," you are not yet ready for downhill racing.

In learning to ski fast, you have to ski fast—at the farthest limits of your control. But choose at first a smooth, uncrowded slope rather than the hairiest stretch of an expert racing trail. Take the lowest possible crouch on a long gentle slope and see how long you can hold it. Pushing down hard with your feet after each little bump you can feel how you increase your speed. Race down such a slope with a group of friends, testing both your wax job and your crouch position.

The next step is to work out on rougher terrain, pulling your turns out long as you ride the bumps; swinging from one high-speed turn into the other; letting your edges carve the turn rather than skid; and trying in particular to find that relaxed, resilient stance you must have if you are not to be thrown by sharp bumps.

Skiing fast over bumps, you will make two discoveries:
1. *How to let the bump unweight your skis* so that with a minimum of effort you can begin to carve your turn.
2. How to straighten your legs and make your edges bite as you complete your turn on the down side of a fall-away corner.

The action of edging your skis and straightening your legs comes naturally at the conclusion of your turn. It is part of the "unwinding" process which automatically leads into the unweighting, rotation, and angulation of the next turn. The importance of this phase of the modern turn may not have been apparent when you were first learning, going cautiously down an easy slope. But when you are going fast, it is life insurance to you: it (and sharp edges) may be all that keeps you on the course and out of the woods.

The final phase of training for downhill comes in the mastery of running multiple bumps, and of pre-jumping a variety of rolls and pitches. Needless to say you will probably already be racing and discovering for yourself the things you cannot yet handle at high speeds. No one can tell you how to take a particular terrain problem in racing.

*Training
for
Downhill
Racing*

Your own judgment is the only guide, and a trial at racing speeds the only test.

Three further points about training for downhill may help:
1. Always ski in control. Confidence has as much to do with balance as does a good nervous system, and most falls at high speed come as the result of sitting back through lack of confidence.
2. Ski in all conditions of snow—at the sides of the trail, in powder or rough, broken snow, over the worst bumps you can find. It is necessary training for the eye and the mind as well as the body.
3. The tougher the conditions the more aggressively you must ski.

Memorizing a Downhill Course

The "line" is as wide as your two skis and runs from the start of the course to the finish. The shortest line in time is often not the straightest. The best line is the smoothest and shortest you can hold.

That line is a secret which even you, at first, do not know. Your first step, therefore, in memorizing a downhill course is to ski it slowly, sideslipping and stopping here and there to study what's above and what's below. Your first choice must be a path five to ten feet wide down the course which takes in the control gates and allows for the principal bumps and angles, the main pitches and flats.

All courses have spots of major difficulty and others of comparative rest. You next run the course in these obvious sections, stopping after each one to determine how you might have run it better and to watch how others run it. On the third time down, you run the course at nearly top speed, wind-checking when you need to slow down, and stopping only infrequently.

There are certain to be critical areas in the course where an edge-check or a wind-check may actually save you time. When you know these spots in detail, run the course nonstop several times, always staying in control but increasing your speed wherever you can squeeze out another tenth of a second. Your ideal line is now narrowed to less than a foot in width, but you are familiar with the wider area in case you can't ride this line exactly. Though other skiers may seem to be going faster, this is your line. In practice, stretch your luck a little. You may fall. It's humiliating, but that is all; if you never fall, you are not skiing fast enough.

Checks? Forget about the other skiers. Check where a check is called for in your mind. Someone may try the worst part of the trail without a check, and he may hold it. But you must ski on your skis. *You should be thinking during the race, not of checks, but of speed.* How does the speed feel? How much can you handle? How much of a turn must you put in to have the right speed over a difficult obstacle?

Then consider: What time is the race set for? What will the snow be like at starting time? What will the course be like if the weather turns cold? Or warm? Or it begins to snow? You need to know these things, for they determine both how you will wax and how you will vary your line.

After that, relax. Don't let your imagination race the course bump by bump all night. Your memory will come back at start time.

Starting

Races can depend on the tenth part of a second and so it is often said that they are won right at the start. The start, in this sense, includes not only the line the skier must cross but the first forty or fifty yards of the course during which the racer must achieve a maximum acceleration. The method of starting must vary with the terrain. Sometimes you can plant both poles securely near the actual starting line and be ready to lean forward for the initial thrust. Sometimes, as with a flat first slope, it is better to have one pole planted a little back of the other.

By the time the "ten seconds" call is given you should be all set in the gate, relaxing. Then as the starter begins the final count—"Five . . . four . . . three"—you listen intently for its rhythm. As he says "One!" you have just a second: you lean forward on your poles, out over the starting line. At "Go!" you explode from your tottering position. If you have caught the rhythm of the count exactly, your start will be perfect, but it behooves you not to try to shave the gun by a fraction of a second, for it is your responsibility entirely if you are early and have to be shouted back.

Many racers plunge off a starting gate into a skating start, believing that this will gain them speed the quickest. Yet skating with skis is a clumsy motion at slow speeds, a motion skaters themselves do not use at a start, and it is doubtful that a skating start, under most conditions, is as good as three or four short vigorous pole strokes followed by a racing crouch.

The above description of a start deals only with the simple mechanics. There are at least three other elements which are important in subtracting seconds from your time. The first of these is the training period during which you work out all the details of your line, and in particular memorize the first stretch, the first main obstacles, for these you will be hitting when you are not yet entirely warmed up to the business of racing. The second element is a good wax job, the details of which you will find in the Appendix, p. 173.

The third element of a good racing start is a proper warm-up period just prior to answering your number at the line. For this you should allow at least a half hour. You may find the snow conditions at the top quite different from what you expected. You may have to add some wax, or even, with bad luck, to scrape off everything you so carefully painted on.

Fifteen minutes before your starting time you should be tightening your boots in the warming hut at the top of the course. You know every bump, how you will push down on the far side of some to gain more speed, how you will jump and pre-jump others, where you will crouch and where wind-check. The hasty edge-checks you will make are still a matter of some doubt, which cannot be resolved in warming-hut meditations. You may have to check—but how much? That will depend on how the snow feels, how the speed feels when you are actually on the course. You know by now how fast you can pass over the critical points of the course, but you do not yet know what speed you will have as you come into these critical points.

Boots on, do some slow deep-knee bends and other stretching exercises. Then put on your skis, side step quickly up the slope above the start and run down several times at full speed until your muscles are warm and eagerness is in your blood.

Then it is time. Sideslip to the start, unzip your warm-up pants and jacket. Pull your amber goggles away from your face until the mist on them clears. "Ten seconds." You breathe easily now. Now, there is only one man and one course. . . .

Racing
Too Soon
and Too Much

This chapter on downhill running and racing would not be complete without a few words about competition and its relation to general skiing. Americans tend to be impatient to get on with the finding of new champions; more good racers will be made, they believe, if there are more big races. And so the schedule for the winter months is jammed to bursting with competitions; neither competitors nor officials have a moment in which to relax and enjoy skiing. This frantic program sends its shock waves down to the youngest children. In snow country it is not unusual to find youngsters of eight or ten already wearing crash helmets and chafing at the start like hopped-up head-hunters.

There is a fallacy here. Racing does not necessarily produce good skiers. Racing will confirm as many bad habits in skiing as it will produce good ones. It diverts attention from learning to ski well to learning to ski fast.

Whatever the values of racing—and there are many—this much can be said: skill should come first, racing after. Not vice versa. The young skier who goes out to learn nothing but skiing, and nothing but the best—feet together, under all conditions of snow, ice, bumps, powder, wind pack, corn—will almost certainly be better in the end than the boy who spends his weekends racing.

And this can also be said: that all-round skiing should come first, specialization after. Few people remember that Buddy Werner was once a fine junior jumper. He skis the way he does now partly because the jumper is still in him. The same could be said of Dick Durrance, Barney McLean, Gordy Wren, and many others.

The spectacle of modern high-school racing is particularly night-marish: every weekend a meet; three or four events jammed into one day; no time to study the courses; no time to wax; no time to relax; no time to train; youngsters with no technique at all bashing their way through the slalom gates, cursing their way around cross-country courses; youngsters popeyed with fear bumping off some quarry called a jump, which has not been properly designed or kept in shape. All for the so-called sake of the team.

If we had time to stop and start over, would we not say: "Skiing must first be fun! Jumping, for the fun of it, for the instinct and confidence it develops. Slalom, for the fun of it, for the precision it teaches. And picnic tours, for the open country and the open heart. After that, later, the races."

Racing Staleness

A second problem related to racing is staleness, of the old-fashioned variety. It happens to all skiers in a mild way at the end of the ski season. But it comes as an acute collapse of interest among those who race too much. The disease of staleness—for those who go to Europe for a season of racing—may border on a temporary psychosis.

And no wonder. The young, ambitious racer, flying out of Winter Park, or Putney, or McCall, to Zurich and St. Anton (where the Swiss, Italians, French, and Austrians are in training for a world championships) is setting himself up for the most stunning shock of his career. On his first morning out, in the sportiest togs he can shrink himself into, full of confidence and American records, he strides out to the practice slope . . . and then it hits him: twenty-five skiers tearing through a slalom better than anyone he has ever seen before . . . better than he had ever imagined possible!

That ghastly first sight is his finish. Haunted by the vision of those whizzing bodies which never seem to make a mistake, he skis and skis and skis, practices, practices, practices, talks technique, changes technique, changes skis, eats whale meat and yogurt, and has nightmares of jumbled slalom poles.

In short, he kills himself with what he calls "training." Far more important than a few last desperate wiggles through an offset-Allais flush is the *eagerness* to ski which comes only to a rested body and mind. Often in racing it is that last bit of strength that makes the difference between falling and not falling. That last strength must come from a reserve which no longer exists in an overtrained body.

Cross-country runners gauge their training by following their weight and their pulse rates. The alpine specialists, more subject to psychological influences, have another yardstick which stated simply is: *When in doubt about training, say No!* Don't begin to rationalize; that can go on forever. Quit skiing and ski resorts and ski chatter altogether. Leave them for several days, or a week or two, until the spirit is back.

All of which is to say that skiing is nothing if it is not fun. And this is true of racing, too.

91

THE RACING CROUCH

Standard Crouch

The streamlined position of a racer. The feet are slightly apart when running straight over bumps at high speed.

Variations of Racing Crouch

a. Higher but more restful

b. Arms lowered and apart for bumpy terrain

c. Forward for great speed

d. Weight back on flats

Bud Werner in the racing crouch

High Speed Turn in a Crouch

Where a crouch means everything—stay with it!
This long turn looks unorthodox—but with speed the shovels
of your skis pull you around. You have to rock up on your
edges, and lean forward. With your weight on the outside ski,
and with follow-through from your outside arm, you ride
your edges around an extended corner.

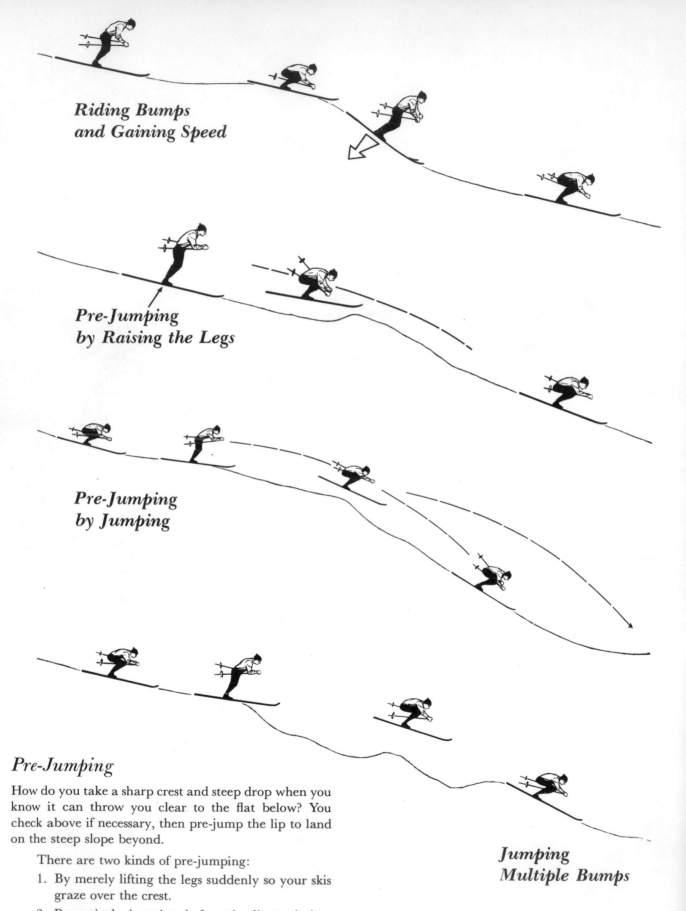

Riding Bumps
and Gaining Speed

Pre-Jumping
by Raising the Legs

Pre-Jumping
by Jumping

Pre-Jumping

How do you take a sharp crest and steep drop when you know it can throw you clear to the flat below? You check above if necessary, then pre-jump the lip to land on the steep slope beyond.

There are two kinds of pre-jumping:
1. By merely lifting the legs suddenly so your skis graze over the crest.
2. By actively jumping before the lip and then pulling your legs up.

Timing is everything. If you jump too late you fly off into space. If you jump too early you ricochet from the lip.

Jumping
Multiple Bumps

For short sharp bumps—pre-jump by lifting the legs.

For long rolling knolls, or steep pitches—pre-jump by actually jumping ahead of the lip.

R. Miller off "Niagra" at the National Downhill Championships in Aspen, Colorado. Having made a good prejump the skier maintains his crouch over a long flight.

Josl Rieder of Austria

Slalom

Slalom is a dance, an intricate ballet, a saber dance on steel edges. While not the hair-raising spectacle that jumping or downhill is, slalom takes full measure of a man's skill under maximum pressure. The slightest miscalculation in speed, momentum, skid, balance, edge control can lead to an awful tangle with the poles—and harsh judgment from the court of stop watches.

The race itself is a monument to the imagination and persistence of one man: Arnold Lunn. Seer and organizer of the early British developments of Mürren and Wengen, Lunn's interest in slalom grew spontaneously, as it did in this country, out of earlier attempts to hold proficiency tests in the various turns and maneuvers of skiing. Lunn chanced upon an old Norwegian flag race—the slalaam—which had been tried and discarded years before, and he saw at once its potentialities for the great test of skill it has become. It was his innovation to use two flags together instead of one—pairs of flags set so as to make use of the slope's most interesting terrain features.

Lunn began to experiment and to write. His mastery of technical problems of slalom was matched by his prose; he literally forced the Scandinavians to take back their foundling, which he had adopted and raised to promising youth. After years of doubts and resistance, slalom was accepted as a legitimate ski race, included in the F. I. S. championships in 1933, and in the Olympics of 1936.

Americans took readily to Lunn's slalom. The first race was held at the Dartmouth Winter Carnival in 1925 when Professor Charles Proctor, with Lunn's articles in hand, laid out the course, trained a team of ex-telemark specialists, and instructed the first bewildered gatekeepers in their incomprehensible duties.

Notes for Beginners

While slalom is generally thought to be the business of racers only, there is no better teaching device for intermediate skiers nor any better game for children. As with any teaching device, it can be overworked, or its value largely destroyed through the use of cramped and crabbed sets of gates. Nevertheless, anyone wanting to learn precision and control and a fluid style in skiing should occasionally take a dozen pairs of flags to some out-of-the-way corner of a ski slope and practice slalom.

Begin simply. Try a series of open gates. Note how you can, by shifting the gates a few feet, create or destroy the fluid nature of a good course. Experiment next with bumps: placing the gate on top of the bump, above the bump, below the bump, to the inside, and to the outside of the bump. Here are five new variables in one gate.

Next try closed gates and hairpins and flushes. Each one introduces new problems; each one offers at least the choice of two "lines"; and by staggering the gates or offsetting them or turning them obliquely, new and more complex situations can be laid out. Thus with only the simplest gates, and using the potentialities of the slope, you can create a wide variety of ski problems.

Slalom is not a matter of learning a new way to ski, only of applying the skills you already know. Open gates are sweeping turns; closed gates and hairpins test preciseness and the conservation of speed; flushes are enforced wedeln. Festops you will need, and sideslips, abstem wedeln, and even pole jumps. The kick turn (believe it or not) is sometimes seen in Olympic races when a runner has overreached himself.

In learning to run slalom there are a few general rules which may be of help to you:
1. Set only a few gates at a time, not a whole hillside pincushioned with flags, and *strive for smoothness and accuracy first, speed later.*

2. Stay "high" on most gates and complete your turn before entering, holding as close to the upper or inside pole as you can. (By completing your turn ahead of the gate, you are in full control and already plotting your course for the gates to come.)
3. Go in slow and come out fast. Then go in fast and come out faster.
4. Run straight, feet together, until you have to check; then check hard —rather than slither for 50 feet timidly into your turn.
5. Link your turns into one continuous motion and try to "carve" the turns rather than skid them.
6. Avoid the most common fault—sitting back riding your inside ski.

Slalom Racing

You have to learn to *think ahead* one, two, or three gates. Later you will come to feel how the whole run is one motion from top to bottom. Training the eye to see, the mind to judge, and the body to act is the very basis of skill. It will take time; you will make many mistakes and have much fun.

Slalom skiers training for racing can easily give the wrong impression of slalom, owing to the hectic way they train. To the average skier, slalom racers, practicing, seem like madmen, a loose collection of arms and legs smashing their way to a new world record of violent miscoordination. But there is more than madness in the method. Slalom racers have to practice at maximum speeds. They have to train psychologically for racing at the same time they are sharpening their race techniques. They are pushing themselves beyond the limits of their belief into the possibility of new limits. . . .

But as with training in any athletic event, slalom training must build up from a solid base of skill toward speed and timing.

A good program would follow some such progression as this:
1. *In the first days and weeks train over limited segments of a course, running at reduced speed and working for precision.*
> *a.* a series of open gates
> *b.* a ten-gate flush
> *c.* a series of hairpin turns

Such abbreviated sections of a course are valuable to start on because they allow you to observe yourself and to study other skiers under limited conditions. It takes a while for the body to remember just how it feels to run slalom. To correct one error at a time is all that any skier can do.
2. *Next, train for speed over the same short courses.*
> When smoothness and control are coming, when your turns are where you want them, your line close to the poles—then bomb it! If smoothness vanishes, go back to a somewhat slower speed. There

will often be times, in a particular set of gates, when there is a choice between a slower, safer line and a faster, more difficult line. Always take the faster line and work at it until it lets you through.

Once you have mastered running these short courses at full speed, it will be time to:

3. *Train on a nearly full-length course.*

This is what you are practicing for—a racing course. You must be willing to meet the requirements of a slalom race: a full racing start, frantic poling between gates, and no stopping until the bottom. You may fall. Get up, keep going. It is really necessary training in recovery. Maybe the practice will squeak you through in an important race. Whatever happens, keep going. You have to train yourself to the maximum urgency of race conditions. Thus do champions learn not only to beat all others but to exceed themselves.

A slalom workout over a simulated course such as outlined above is necessarily intense and therefore should be brief. An hour twice a day is plenty. And, once the racing season has begun, two workouts a week are sufficient. As with training for downhill racing, if you are worried about "how you look," you are not yet ready for racing. The stop watch does not recognize form, except as good form makes possible greater speed.

Everything that has to do with preparations, training, starting, checking, gaining speed on the bumps and flats, as mentioned in the chapter on Downhill Skiing, holds true in slalom races, even though the events are radically different. The question of racing staleness is also appropriate. One thing, however, is slightly different: *memorizing the course.* The slalom runner cannot train on the actual race course, as the downhill runner does, but he has the benefit of studying the course in every detail as he walks up it. The slalom runner, of course, will be measured against time, but his real problem is accuracy. His judgment and his memory must be flawless. He may gain a few shavings of a second skiing out of turns and poling on the flats, but to overshoot one gate, or lose the rhythm of a flush, or misjudge the effect of ice or bumps or bathtubs can cost him whole seconds.

And so slalom runners memorize their courses from the bottom up: looking up, looking down, moving slowly, standing in their exact lines, looking up, looking down, estimating, recalculating, rehearsing. As they climb higher, they must constantly revise and refine their plans, for a set of gates seen from above looks quite different from the way it did, a moment earlier, seen from below. In most courses there are two or three critical sets of gates. These tricky combinations require the hardest decisions as to "line," but it is rare that a race is actually won or lost here. In general, races are won or lost in the many open gates which make up the bulk of the course.

Sometimes the fastest way to take a particular set or combination is not the best way, owing to the gates below. However, when there is a clear choice of a safer way and a more exacting but faster line, as in training, choose the faster line—and concentrate to make it pay off. You will never be satisfied if you play it safe and come out second.

The Open Gate

The open gate! How deceptively simple it is.
What could be easier than turning around a pole?
This most common slalom problem is what races
are made of, where they are won and lost.

Set up four or five gates and run them first for smoothness. Stay high. Make your approach high, turn and get up under the inside pole in order to be high for the next gate. This is what the reverse shoulder was invented for.

As with wedeln and mambo the swing of one turn ends in the preparation for the next.

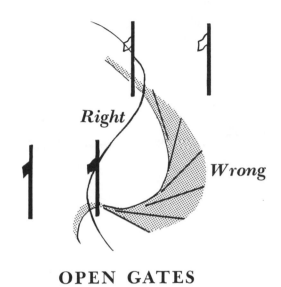

Right

Wrong

OPEN GATES

Poling and Skating Out of Open Gate

A good slalom rule for almost any set of gates is: go in relatively slowly and come out fast. While the rule does not always hold, the reverse never holds. "Fast" means as fast as is right for the next set of gates and the rest of the course.

Three things combine to give a good slalom runner his speed:

1. Skillful edge-control.
2. Skating out of the last part of the turns.
3. Drive with the poles.

Note the reach and drive and timing of these pole thrusts as the skier skates out of the gate.

Closed Gates

Squeeze through. Don't rock way up on your edges; carve your turns smoothly and don't turn more than you have to to squeeze through.

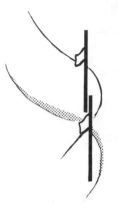

Both Right

Both Wrong

No skidding, then pole, pole, pole. I looks frantic in a race, or in practice but underlying the effort is precision and timing.

You see poles, edges, turns—yes. Bu do you still see unweighting, rotation angulation in these pictures?

Hairpin

The hairpin is a nice test of judgment and control, designed to let you over-reach yourself by coming into the upper gate too fast, then skidding too much in the turn, or falling below the second gate.

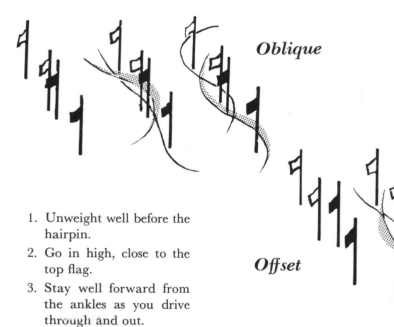

Oblique

Offset

1. Unweight well before the hairpin.
2. Go in high, close to the top flag.
3. Stay well forward from the ankles as you drive through and out.

The practical value—the necessity—of unweighting, rotation, angulation is clearly shown in these pictures.

The Flush

"A flush is enforced wedeln."

1. In high . . .
2. . . . Squeezing through . . .
3. . . . and out . . . next is a . . .

There are eight different paths you can trace through a three-gate flush, but only one will be the fastest for a given set. In most cases think of the flush as an S-turn: festop, one, two, pole, pole, pole.

When you can come out the bottom of a flush in as good control as when you went in, set some variations:

1. Try a 5-gate flush down a steep pitch.
2. Set a 5-gate flush over bumps.
3. Try a 10-gate flush.

Increase your tempo with each run—pushing your limits
beyond what you believe you can do.
Checking must be instantaneous and accurate. Don't
start your check forty feet above the first gate and then
drift cautiously up to it. Ski at top speed, check hard,
then dive into the combination as fast as possible and
come out faster.

Five Gate Oblique Flush

Christian Pravda slicing through a fast hairpin

H. CLAUSING, GARMISCH, GERMANY

CHAPTER 7

The High-speed Turn
and Crouch
Edge-control
Children's Races and
All-round Skiing

Giant Slalom

Giant slalom was first conceived as a race which would combine some of the best points of slalom and downhill and yet rule out some of the obvious dangers of the latter. However, it has not supplanted the straight race; instead, it has been recognized as having merits peculiarly its own. The modern giant slalom, therefore, is neither a controlled downhill race nor a wide-open slalom, and should not be thought of in these terms by racers or course-setters.

A comparison with the other alpine events may help to make clear the differences:

	Minimum vertical drop (Olympic)	Average No. of gates	Average speed
Slalom	617 feet	60	15 mph.
Giant slalom	1,234 feet	35	30 mph.
Downhill	2,468 feet	as required	50 mph.

Unfortunately giant slalom has been largely neglected in this country. Partly this is due to the fact that it must be "another event" in an already hectic weekend racing schedule. Partly it is due to a lack of terrain suitable for training. In the eastern part of the United States, with its wooded and populous trails, the runner rarely gets above 35 m.p.h. To train at 50 m.p.h. would be suicide or manslaughter. And in the West, where there are open mountains to train on, the skier can rarely find the bumps, gullies, rolls, and pitches which make a good practice slope. A giant-slalom hill needs to be long and wide, rolling, steep but variable so that many choices are available and many techniques can be tested: jumping, pre-jumping, crouching, skating out of turns, riding airborne over multiple bumps, making long smooth turns . . . always at high speeds.

Training for and racing giant slalom follows much the same plan as that set forth in the chapters on Downhill and Slalom. Only one important technicality needs to be mentioned here: *filing the edges.* Your edges should always be sharp—this is as true for skiers as it is for skaters. It takes but a few minutes to hone your edges (as described in the section on Waxing) yet it would be folly, if you have dull edges, to sharpen them a few minutes before the start of a race. Such an action can radically alter the checking characteristics of your skis just when you need to know exactly how they will behave. *Burring* the edges over with a butcher's steel, a popular pre-race ritual a few years ago, is even more dangerous. Burred edges grab on ice in a most disconcerting way. They may line you into the trees or into a sudden fall; at the very least they make impossible the subtle sliding-slicing sequences which constitute good edge-control.

Edge-Control   The greatest giant-slalom performer in recent times was Toni Sailer. During the final four years of his racing career he won every major giant slalom he entered—and by several seconds! What was his secret? The answer lies in the finesse with which he handled high-speed turns. Sailer was able, better than any of his rivals, to carve his turns where he wanted them in order to squeeze out the last bit of speed; he was able to hold a moderate racing crouch throughout the course, thus reducing his wind resistance to an absolute minimum; and he had an uncanny sense of just when and how much to make his edges bite.

Fine edge-control is almost the *sine qua non* of expert alpine skiing. More than any other factor—courage, equipment, wax—it is edge-control which separates the good racer from the good skier. It is a skill centered mainly in the ankles: your ankles must be able to feel what your edges are doing and know at once how to carve or slip a turn or cling to a fall-away corner.

116

Much has already been said on this subject. Learning to make good use of the edges began right at the beginning, with the snowplow turns and slideslips. More determined use came instinctively with better technique: the Festop, the modern turn, checking, the high-speed long-radius turn, etc. But in learning these standard maneuvers, you had to concentrate on the motions of the whole body—unweighting, rotation, angulation—on the gross architecture of the turn itself. Now it is time to consider just the steel edges, as a Japanese artist would consider the tip of his brush.

With the expert skier the slightest movement of the shoulders, hips, ankles, transmitted to the edges, is sufficient to carve those long smooth crescents in hard-packed snow, over bumps and rutted pitches. It is a craft so cunning as to be almost imperceptible.

Here are a few exercises to make you more fully acquainted with your edges:

1. Stand on one ski and rock up first on one edge, then on the other. Try the same exercise while moving on one ski.
2. Skate on the flat or down a gentle slope, making long easy strokes, as a racing skater would.
3. On a steeper slope sideslip straight down the fall-line, sideways— slow, fast, slow, stop, fast, etc.—controlling your speed by the bite you give to your edges. Then, feet together, sideslip forward, rock back, then forward again.
4. Do a series of abrupt edge stops from a forward sideslip. Then a series of hard Festops. Then wedeln.
5. Try making a full turn on just the inside edge of the outside ski, and the "butterfly" of the glamorous ski instructors, a turn on the outside edge of the inside ski.
6. Traveling 20 to 30 m.p.h. down a moderate slope, suddenly throw your skis directly sideways (as you would in an emergency stop). As you slide to a stop, first make the edges bite, then let them drift into a slide again.
7. Choosing an area where there are many small bumps, run it obliquely or in long turns at 30 to 40 m.p.h., *pushing down hard on the downside of each bump* to keep your edges carving. This is the most difficult and most important of giant-slalom maneuvers. For the recreational skier the ability to keep a turn carving on the downside of a bump may save him in a close brush with trees; for the racer, it can save him many seconds wasted in slithering and checking.

Most of the above exercises are not new. They are reviewed here in order to emphasize what was not possible fully to describe earlier, the importance of edge-control. Concentrate on holding your skis firmly together, and in making the turns (items 4 and 7) let the outside ski carry two thirds of your weight. These exercises will not teach you to be an Olympic racer, but they will help you to "feel" your edges working, as much a living part of you as the finger tips are for a rock climber.

The pictures that follow were taken of some of the world's best skiers in action in Giant Slalom races. You can only guess at their speeds, but you can clearly see the semi-crouched racing position, legs quite straight, and you will notice how, in a well-designed ski, both the bite of the edges and the bend of the ski combine to carve out those long-radius turns which are the envy of all alpine skiers.

Children's Races and All-Round Skiing
Giant slalom has a special value for children which deserves mention: it is the ideal device for *teaching good downhill techniques.* Slalom is often too icy, cramped, and intricate for a child to comprehend or manage, while aimless running down the standard downhill trails may teach little more than how to go fast with slovenly technique. But in giant slalom the best terrain features of a particular slope can be put to work. Speed and bumps come under the persuasive demands of flags. Judgment, quick decision, accuracy and control are tested at every gate, while the fluid unity of the course, the sense that a good run is one continuous action from top to bottom, develops quite naturally. To the young skier giant slalom has the "feel" of downhill in it. What is more important still: it is fun!

One cannot overemphasize the value of a broad general development of skiing skills in a child's early years. The broader the foundation the higher the final pyramid of specialization.

An ideal training program for young skiers would be oriented in some such way as this:

Grade-school age:	Giant slalom
	Jump
Junior-high age:	Giant slalom
	Slalom
	Jump
High-school age:	Downhill
	Slalom
	Cross-country
	Jump
College age:	Specialization

The purpose of such a program is twofold: (1) it brings out a mastery of control and technique first, speed later; and (2) it promotes all-round skiing skills before specialization.

118

There is no doubt whatever that jumping is best learned young (and on small hills) when the child skis naturally and easily, without undue fear or self-consciousness and before alpine habits become too strong. There can be no doubt that jumping experience contributes greatly to the perfection of alpine techniques. In the same way the self-discipline and hardy enduring qualities which are brought out in cross-country racing have something directly to do with an alpine skier's ability to give that little bit more than his all which makes the difference, whatever the race. And this is not to mention the pleasures of ski mountaineering and touring which are always open, after the racing days, to those who have learned the simple art of cross-country skiing.

Racing events are obviously quite different. The jumper, for example, packs the whole of his existence into 3 or 4 seconds of flight, while the cross-country runner may run for three and a half hours, uphill and down—and love it; downhill is almost as different from slalom as hockey is from fancy skating. Each race demands special qualities, physical and psychological. The downhill runners and jumpers tend to be devil-may-care extroverts; the cross-country racers are Spartans; the slalom experts are, above all, ballet artists.

There would seem to be little logic, then, in the so-called "paper races" or "combined events" (slalom and downhill; jumping and cross-country). Yet the combined events—like the 4-way Ski Meisterschaft —give voice to a fundamental belief that it is wise and good to foster all-round skiing. The specialists will, of course, top the list in any major competition. But that is not the point. Specialists will come up automatically from the ranks of young talented skiers. The point is that the specialists with a broad background in skiing will almost always be better than those who have restricted their development too early.

Skiers have a favored brotherhood, one that lasts a lifetime and which leaps over all national boundaries. Yet when from among their group a truly great all-round skier emerges—a Sigmund or a Birger Ruud, a Dick Durrance, a Gordy Wren—then even the specialists themselves must give way before these finest practitioners of the sport.

The hunting look,
the cutting edge . . .

Josl Rieder, Austria

ni Sailer, Austria. The greatest of
odern Alpine skiers

WOLFGANG LERT PHO

Cross-Country Racing

"Of the four different events characterizing the competitive side of skiing you might say that jumping is the most spectacular, downhill the fastest and most dangerous, slalom the most graceful, and cross-country the hardest."

That quotation describes the various ski events and is fair enough as far as it goes. But it notes only the external aspects, giving little hint as to the true rewards of competition. This is especially true of cross-country racing. It is "hard" in the sense that the body and mind of the good skier must be trained tough, must be trained beyond toughness actually to enjoy and take pride in the rigors of running. But how much more is there to the event than simply being hard! How much pleasure is there in finding one's body—that remarkable machine—able to do such work with ease and efficiency. How much joy in learning to handle the technical details of running with smoothness. And

123

how many lifelong friendships tempered in the fires of competition. . . . Only the good runner who has gotten beyond fighting himself on the long courses can say.

In the North European countries, where cross-country skiing is the natural way of walking in winter, cross-country racing is probably the most popular form of competition. Ten to twenty thousand spectators are not uncommon at such competitions as the Holmenkollen in Norway or the Salpausselka in Finland. At a recent "Vassalop" (which commemorates the birth of modern Sweden) 750 racers were at the start for the 85-km. race. The national heroes of those northern countries are men like "Mora Nisse" Karlson, Saarinen, Utterstrom, Bergendahl, Brodahl—men held in the same regard as Ruth, Gehrig, Cobb and others in this country.

The recent Olympic Winter Games at Squaw Valley, California, testify to the great tradition of cross-country racing: running events made up exactly half of all ski races; the events ranging from 5 km. to 50 km. in length. Owing to the recent growth of alpine skiing in this country, a fact commonly forgotten is that in the first three Olympic Winter Games cross-country and jumping were the only ski events held. The alpine races had not developed to a point where they qualified as Olympic competition until 1936.

In modern times even the well-established nordic races have changed enormously: tracks are cleared and groomed, packed and flagged, as carefully as a slalom course; skis are light and fragile; boots are scarcely heavier than Oxfords; and the business of training and waxing has become as much a science as an art. It is not the day of the "lumberjack" any more. City boys with training and the techniques of speed can match seconds with their more rugged country cousins. Cross-country and nordic combined events are races in which Americans can learn to excel if they once discover the fun of good running.

Elementary Techniques

The idea that skiing is a "form of walking or sliding on snow" obviously has a more than general application to the sport of cross-country racing. "Technique" here is quite simply a matter of learning the most efficient way to walk, slide, or run on skis. Speed is the final measure, and everything from a runner's psychological make-up down to the wax on his skis and the food in his stomach has a bearing on his speed. Yet first things must come first: before a runner can effectively use the more advanced techniques, he must have mastered those forms of locomotion most closely related to walking. There are no true short cuts. As the swimmer, through swimming several hundred miles of a crawl stroke, smooths out his motions, co-ordinates his breathing and timing, so the cross-country runner must put the miles behind him before he will know what technique is. Books, charts, photographs, training films and training tables can make that work intelligent, but that distance—hundreds of miles running on skis—must also be there.

Have you ever noticed when walking that it is the right arm and left leg that work together, and the left arm and the right leg? The opposite sides of the body are co-ordinated. Single poling—the most basic technique—follows this principle. The opposite arm and leg are working together, as in walking, and the poles are useful extensions of the arm which increase propulsion. This is the natural way to ski, and the one used at least 75 per cent of the time even by our best racers.

Diagonal (or Single) Poling

What is it that constitutes good technique? Basically it is four important actions working in harmony:

1. A running position and timing which can convert the kick and pole thrust into a large forward component, and which does not exhaust the runner with a sinking and rising motion of the body.
2. Drive with the poles.
3. A short sharp "kick" properly timed in the stride and of maximum strength.
4. A rhythm and action which give relaxation between moments of effort.

Body Position: The term "half crouch" best describes the body position necessary for cross-country skiing. The position must of necessity be one of relaxation in order to give the strongest and quickest reactions possible over the duration of the race. As is evident in the adjoining photo, the back and lower leg are approximately parallel. The appearance is that of readiness from which the racer can exert the strongest possible downward force when "kicking."

Kick: The experienced racer knows how to adjust his technique

(kick) to the many changing conditions confronting the runner. Whatever the snow, the kick is basically the same: it is the principal force giving the body forward motion. Technically, the kick is started directly under the body—*not behind it*—at the moment when the feet pass each other. The direction of the kick is mainly downward, not backward, which is contrary to the belief of many. It is an instantaneous snap of the hip, leg, and ankle, resulting in a complete stretching of the leg. Kicking downward provides for a more confident, stronger kick than kicking backwards, for it gives the running wax a maximum of grip on the snow, besides insuring proper timing of the kick. The backward kick tends toward lateness as well as a tendency to drop the hips. If the kick is executed properly, the body will naturally go in the opposite direction or upward. The body is not carried through any great vertical distance; the recovery phase of the poling motion keeps this to a minimum. Maximum force can thus be exerted in the shortest period of time.

Poling—Recovery Phase: You are now faced with the question of how to keep the head and shoulders generally on an even plane, thus reducing the vertical motion of the body resulting from the kick. The key lies in the proper action of the arms and poles when going forward. The arms are simply brought forward in a normal rhythmical motion as in walking. The driving force of the diagonal technique comes from the proper execution of this movement. The arm is relaxed on the completion of its rearward motion and is swung forward along its natural arc, creating, due to its centrifugal force, a tremendous amount of forward drive. This forward motion is not a stiff, jerky motion; quite the contrary, its smoothness is essential to the rhythm of the entire body in running.

Note from the adjacent photo the angle of the pole when its point hits the snow in respect to the racer's over-all body position and particularly the position of the opposite foot. Correct pole length is clearly of utmost importance. A pole that is too tall will undoubtedly take you out of your normal easy running position. Reaching too high, you will lose both rhythm and thrust. Compare the driving action so evident in the preceding photograph with that of the picture at the right. Here the skier has no forward drive with the upper body. This deadens the whole technique. Remember that the proper motion of the hands is to pass close to the legs as they swing forward in their natural arc, then slightly across the body to their foremost position.

Where and how should the pole be planted? Examine the photos of Kolchin. Note that, when the pole is planted, the skier is *looking directly at the hand.* This is a good rule to follow. It will insure a proper running position in respect to the amount of knee bend. Should the line of sight be appreciably above, or below, the hand, it is safe to assume the body position isn't correct, or the poles not of the right length.

126

Poling—Active Phase: At the completion of the recovery phase the body should be driving forward so that the poling motion is initiated by body weight; thus the heavier muscles of the upper body are brought into play first, saving the lighter muscles of the arm for the last three fourths of the poling motion. The arm should travel backward close to the body, as it did coming forward, in order to work effectively. As you become tired in running, you will notice a tendency for your hand to come back high, above its natural arc, with the elbow winging outward. Remember this and avoid it, for practically all of the useful force which should be imparted by proper poling will become dissipated. The pole is not held or gripped tightly. Even this is tiring—a taut hand leads to a tightening of the whole body. The pole should be held loosely between the thumb and forefinger.

Kick—Recovery Phase: Now that you know how to kick and pole effectively, it is equally significant that you know what to do with the leg after the kick is made. The ski must return to the track as soon as possible to become the gliding ski. *Do not let this leg become straightened* as it goes forward. A straightened leg increases the downward force, thereby increasing the coefficient of friction and causing the ski to stop sliding long before it should. What you have actually done is to simply apply the brakes. Instead, keep the knee pressed forward as long as possible. This will naturally have to be timed to suit your velocity.

The importance of correct knee pressure is well illustrated by Russia's Kolchin pictured at the right. Note how he runs on his toes.

RICHARD ELIOT

His ankles are loose and free, so that the heel of the boot is on the ski only when it is in its foremost position. Note the forward drive in his stride. That is the part that is useful. He brings his arm and pole forward smoothly, in a relaxed easy swing that imparts extra drive into his running.

Common errors associated with the diagonal technique, or single pole, are:

1. Dropping of the hips, which will delay the kick.
2. Bending over from the waist.
3. Weak kick.
4. Allowing the ski to fall back on the track too soon following the kick.
5. No power in the poling motion.
6. Letting the arms swing wide in both the thrust and recovery motions.
7. Straightening the knee of the leg on the gliding ski.

The Diagonal Technique for Hill Climbing

The single-pole technique, as learned in level running, must be slightly modified for running uphill. These are the most significant changes:

1. The body position must not be allowed to fall too far forward.
2. The kick is usually shorter, with less straightening of the leg.
3. The bumps and snow are used to a maximum to ensure grip of the wax.

Body Position: Your main concern so far has been in getting over level ground. What happens when you reach a hill? The answer naturally depends upon the steepness of the hill, your condition, and the wax. Basically, however, if you try to maintain your normal running position, the center of gravity of the body will fall in front of the feet and the skis will tend to slip out from under you, even though properly waxed. To counteract this, drop into a slightly lower running position, letting the knees drive even more forward. This will bring the center of gravity back over your feet and skis.

The Kick: Basically the kick is the same except that the recovery is quicker than in level running. More attention is shifted to the front part of the stride. At this stage of your development you should concern yourself mainly with *keeping as long a stride as possible,* even though the tempo of the cycle may have decreased. Make your skis glide forward, even uphill. If the hill becomes so steep that you cannot slide the skis, simply take as long and fast a step as possible.

The Arms: The arm action is modified from that used in level running. The degree to which the hand holding the pole can come forward is dependent upon the steepness of the terrain. Generally, when the arm is in its forward position, it becomes more bent as the steepness increases. *Remember to get the body weight on top of the poles in order to initiate the poling action.* As the arm swings forward in its normal arc, the hand is still in close to the knee, but lower than when single poling on the flat.

Knee and Ankle: Even more important now than when running on the flat are good knee and ankle action. The body must be loose and relaxed, not struggling with the uphill. Great care must be taken in the placing of the ski; the slightest variation in the terrain and snow surface can make the difference between skis that hold and skis that slip. Let the leg swing loosely, like a pendulum, and do not let the ski hit the snow in back of the body, but directly underneath. As the ski hits and moves forward, the body weight is shifted to it.

"Hill-running" is an art which wins races—with a fast tempo being maintained—but before you can work for speed you must master the rhythm and technique of "hill-skiing." As you undergo this phase in the development of your technique, try to maintain the normal stride as long as possible, *i.e.,* try to keep the skis sliding to the ultimate before shifting over to the 'long-step' (non-gliding) method of hill skiing. You should be able to maintain the normal flat terrain technique until the grade approaches ten to fifteen degrees. Learn to see the opportunities for a solid kick in every bump or change of snow and take full advantage of them.

One phase of technique training many times overlooked is the "double pole." It should be used uphill as well as downhill to allow the upper body to come out of its running position long enough to give certain muscle groups a much needed rest while putting others into use.

Double Poling

Body Position: The major problem in learning this particular technique is getting yourself straightened up (out of the basic diagonal position) so you can double pole effectively. A majority of runners have a tendency to double pole while still in the diagonal position. This does not lead to efficient double poling. Time must be allowed for the body (especially the upper body) to become straightened, but at the same time velocity must be maintained. This is accomplished by taking one, two, or three steps with the feet, the number governed by velocity and terrain. When these steps are taken, it isn't merely a case of "going through the motions," but of taking smooth, aggressive steps. The ankles, knees and hips do not straighten and become rigid, but remain loose and flexible.

Arms: Whether the arms are bent or extended depends a great deal upon the strength of your upper body, and your velocity at the

129

time of double poling. As the preparatory steps are taken, and upper body is simultaneously straightened, the hands are brought upward to a position about twelve inches in front of the face and approximately the same distance apart, with the elbows in a normal position. Again the weight of the body goes on the poles with a powerful drive.

Poling: The reason for starting the pole thrust with the hands near the face is primarily to get the poles in a position where body weight may be brought quickly to bear on them. The poling as always is initiated by body weight, putting the heavier muscles of the back and shoulders to work before the lighter muscles of the arm, which tend to tire more easily. In double poling the lighter muscles are not brought into play until the double-poling motion is at least one half to two thirds of the way through. Note in the accompanying pictures how, when the body weight is brought to bear, the poles are near the vertical. Do not allow the pole tips to swing out in front of you unless your velocity warrants, otherwise you will have to wait for the body to catch up with the poles before any force can be applied. Thus a fraction of a second may be wasted on each stroke. Any attempt to reach out during the initial phase of the double-pole action tends to make the knees, ankles, and hips stiff so the technique will not be effective. The backward drive must be fluid and easy with the body weight applied efficiently to the poles and doing a majority of the work.

Recovery: At the completion of the rearward drive of the poles, the *hips are brought forward,* tending to give an extra impetus to the forward velocity and at the same time bringing the body into position for another double-pole sequence, or one from which single poling may again be resumed.

130

Mistakes commonly associated with the double-poling technique are:

Reaching out too far with the poles, thus causing a delay before a useful force may be imparted to the poling action.

Stiff knees, hips, arms and shoulders—impossible to initiate poling action with body weight. Consequently, a very weak, nonaggressive poling motion.

Stiff knees and too much bend at hips—impossible to follow through correctly with the poles and body. Also difficult to recover from, aggressively, in preparation for the next cycle or shift to other technique.

Skiing Without Poles

Probably the best way to learn the feel of good cross-country technique is to run without poles. It is the key to the development of proper kick, recovery and timing; it shows you just how much you are depending on your poles for balance rather than for forward propulsion; it teaches the all-important "weight shift"; and it forces you to sense with your feet just how much kick your wax can hold. This method of training is so valuable, especially to a beginner, that it should be included in every workout during the first month of ski training, and periodically during the entire season. Thirty minutes of such training is enough, broken up as follows: 10 minutes without poles, 5 minutes with poles, 10 without, 5 with. The monotony may be relieved by hill running and other techniques.

The track is important. It must be well set and frozen in, as little can be learned in running without poles on a soft, sugary track. In the same way the skis must be well waxed to hold so that full attention can be given to the proper motions of running. Early in the season set your track 8 to 12 inches wide on level snow; a quarter-mile loop is enough. As your technique improves, include several small hills in the course. (Racing track width should be 5″ to 6″.) Later, when your kick and balance are developing well, go out on longer courses where you encounter a greater variety of terrain. If natural bumps do not exist in the track, shovel them in. Learning how to keep a loose body and timing your strides to get speed out of bumps are techniques which can save you minutes in a 15-km. race.

Advanced Technique

The Kick and Follow-Through: It is time to examine more exactly what happens in the recovery phase of a stride, after the kick. The ski must not be brought back on the track too soon, normally not until the feet are passing each other. The key to this lies in the proper hip action. The ski will automatically come back on the track too soon without good hip rotation and weight shift. It is impossible for the "square-hipped" skier to follow through.

In recent years there has been much said and written concerning a "high kick." This is simply an immediate relaxation of the kicking leg coupled with the shift and follow-through mentioned above. Too many runners have been working to adopt this high-kick principle without an understanding of the mechanics involved. They make active work out of what should be complete relaxation! The usual error is in attempting the high kick before the kick has been completed.

Needless to say, such a maneuver is worse than worthless. The best runners in the world allow the lower leg to swing up following the kick, and then forward. This you can easily observe from the kick and follow-through of the Russian Kolchin, pictured above, or from Hakulinen of Finland, pictured on the following pages. Mechanically this tends to shorten the length of the leg pendulum, thereby increasing the efficiency of movement in getting the foot forward to its gliding position. The forward drive of the skier on to his gliding ski is usually overlooked, or completely neglected. REMEMBER, the high kick (or recovery) is the relaxation and follow-through after the kick, with care being taken not to allow the ski to hit the track in back of the body.

The Weight Shift: The foregoing action would be impossible without a complete shift of your body weight to the gliding ski. Imagine yourself on a pair of racing skates: the weight, of necessity, must be shifted from side to side so that it is continually over the skate which is in contact with the ice. In cross-country skiing the body weight shifts,

or rolls, to the gliding ski immediately after the kick, working together with the recovery phase of the kick. This so-called roll kick will not be possible if the mid-section of the body is rigid. Relaxation of the hips and torso is essential for proper weight shift. Otherwise you will be skiing "square-hipped" from which position weight shift is impossible. Once your weight has been properly shifted to the gliding ski, you must remember to keep the knee of that leg bent as long as possible to get the most glide out of the kick. Hakulinen, the great Finnish runner, is the beautiful example of the relaxed runner. Study the above photos with care, noting specifically the fine weight shift, and follow-through. Examine hips, shoulders, knees, feet, hands separately as they move through these sequences.

 Body Position: To prevent the ski on the kicking side from coming back on the track prematurely, the upper body will now tend to assume a slightly more upright position. This in itself gives greater comfort and relaxation. It is not a stiffening of the upper body, quite the contrary. The general running position in respect to knee pressure remains the same. But the new position allows for a faster reaction time

134

and a stronger follow-through. It is a natural action, not a forced one, resulting from better weight shift and faster recovery.

Poling—Recovery Phase: Your arm action sets the whole tempo of the diagonal technique. A fast, rhythmic arm action produces a rapid kick, shift, and follow-through. Arm action should therefore slightly precede leg action. *Ease, relaxation, and rapidity in swinging the arm forward is what gives smoothness and power to your whole technique.* It also helps convert the upward motion of a strong downward kick into forward motion. This helps get the body weight out on the gliding ski.

With the upper body raised slightly, the full weight of the body can be used to initiate the poling motion. If there is a question in your mind concerning pole length, use a pole slightly on the short side rather than one too long. A pole too long will do two things:

(a) force the body up out of its natural running position, or

(b) make the forearm come to a nearly vertical position to compensate for the tall pole.

In either case you will not be able to get your weight on top of the pole and your sequence of timing, rhythm, and power will all be lost.

135

Hill
Running
The material presented in Part I dealt primarily with the adjustments necessary for efficient use of level terrain techniques in uphill situations. The "long-stride" system of hill skiing is a sure though slow way to climb. But you are now at a point in your training where, if you want to win races, you must learn to take the hills at a much faster tempo than is possible with the "long stride." The degree to which the tempo may be speeded up depends in large part upon your ability to relax. The stride becomes shorter and faster: it is a continuous rhythm devoid of noticeable stops or hesitations at either end of the stride. The lower leg, from knee to ankle, (the "leg pendulum"), in returning to its forward position, must of necessity shorten its swing. The lower leg, recovering rapidly from the kick, tends naturally to follow a rotary motion, enabling it to drive forward much harder, faster, and smoother. The

136

arms also tend to become more bent in their forward position, though you must keep their forward recovery strong and rhythmically aggressive in order to impart maximum drive into your running. It is generally conceded that a short, faster rhythm on the hills is easier to maintain than the "long stride." The key to hill running is being able to keep a low, loose body position and full knee drive. If you cannot relax, this form of hill running will soon tire you. If so, drop back into the old, long-stride method, still using all the knee drive possible.

Caution: It is customary for one to straighten up out of his running position when fatigue overtakes him. Forward drive then ceases; running becomes a walk. Only good hill-running technique and good training can save you from this difficulty. The photo sequence here illustrates hill running at its best by Sweden's Jernberg. Notice the path taken by the hand as it completes a cycle. And note too his extreme knee pressure.

Study the accompanying photos carefully, from right to left in sequence. This is the change-up as used by Hakulinen going uphill.

The Change-up

Unlike the diagonal, where the opposite pole and leg are working together, the change-up (or "rest-step") utilizes a sequence, which leads to the same foot—same pole combination. This is in direct opposition to the normal co-ordination of the body, consequently it is a hard technique to learn. Little time should be spent on it until you feel you have mastered the single- and double-poling techniques.

Choose a section of your course where the terrain is generally flat, with the track well set and wide enough so the balance will be easy to maintain. Learn to initiate the change-up from either side. Your body co-ordination will probably make the step feel more natural started on one side, but in time you will master it from both sides. The change-up is an intermediate-speed technique.

138

Two Steps: The first two steps taken with the skis are identical with the preparatory phase for double poling, *i.e.,* a two-step during which time the upper body is straightened up out of its normal running position. While this is taking place, the body weight is being shifted so it will end up wholly on the side on which the second step is taken. The pole on this side is merely planted, bent-arm fashion, to catch the balance. There isn't any significant poling action taken with the first step.

Third Step: Meanwhile the arm and leg on the opposite side, now entirely unweighted, are swung forward together. If this is to be executed smoothly and efficiently the upper body must have been raised up during the first two steps, as in the double-poling motion.

Power: The kick and pole thrust work together, although the kick precedes the poling motion. This is the power stroke. The change-up

Sequence of Motions

may be continued in sequence, or you may shift either into a double pole, or back into the diagonal.

Diagrammatically the sequence looks like this:

The Change-Up

Advantages of the "Change-up"

1. It enables you to rest and stretch certain muscle groups while bringing others into use.
2. It is the ideal intermediate-speed technique for use between the normal single- and double-poling techniques.
3. It is ideal for rapid-tempo hill running when immediate adjustments to slight irregularities in terrain are possible.
4. It is useful in adjusting techniques to rough courses with many turns.
5. It is an ideal transitional technique to use when going from level running to hill climbing, and again to get over the top of a hill fast with good relaxation and rest.

Combining Techniques

When you have mastered the change-up, you have a technique for every condition and speed:
1. You have a starting gear—or single pole—for gaining speed.
2. For maintaining speed and slight pick-up you have the change-up.
3. And finally, for high gear, you have the double pole.

Diagrammatically your acceleration techniques look like this:

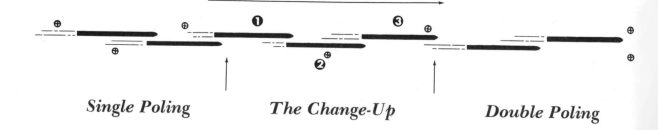

Single Poling   *The Change-Up*   *Double Poling*

Use the whole, or partial combination, whichever the speed and terrain dictate. *You* are the one who must decide which combination is the best.

140

Improper turns may cost you many seconds during a 15-km. race. When you practice technique, do not overlook these simple but important details. They can be practiced between sessions of "no-pole" work thus breaking up the monotony of the latter.

Turning on a Gentle Downhill: Assume your speed is equivalent to, or slightly greater than, a good double-pole speed. As you approach the corner, shift the weight to the outside ski (left ski in the case of the following diagram) and let it carry you into the turn far enough to allow you to assume the new direction when one hard step or skate-step is taken from the outside ski. As soon as the outside ski has been brought into the new direction, finish up the turn by double-poling unless you are already going too fast to double-pole. This type of turn is a good accelerator. One common mistake is not going into the turn far enough before skating off from the outside ski. If you skate off too soon, you will need to make further steps to get around, besides losing the velocity which is obtainable from one good skate-step in the desired direction. Do not straighten and coast around the turn—keep driving.

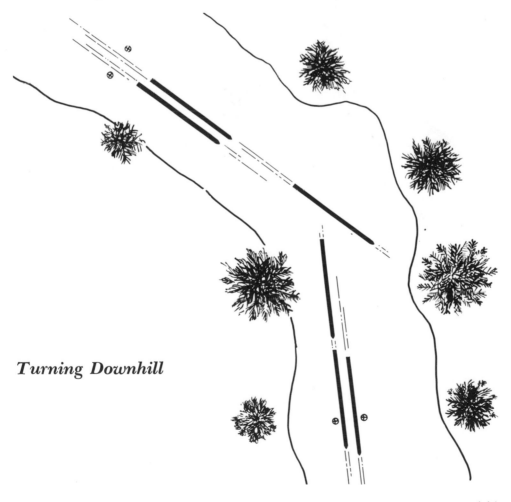

Turning Downhill

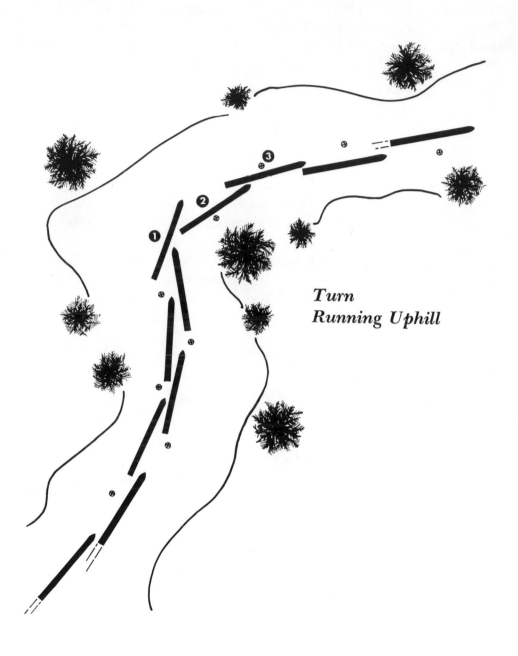

Turn
Running Uphill

Uphill turning: Sharp turns on uphill sections of the course have to be negotiated as quickly and smoothly as possible. Normally such turns are approached with the usual diagonal technique, followed by a skate-step as the means of getting around. While the skate-step is mechanically the same as that previously described, you may not have the necessary velocity to carry you in the new direction. This means

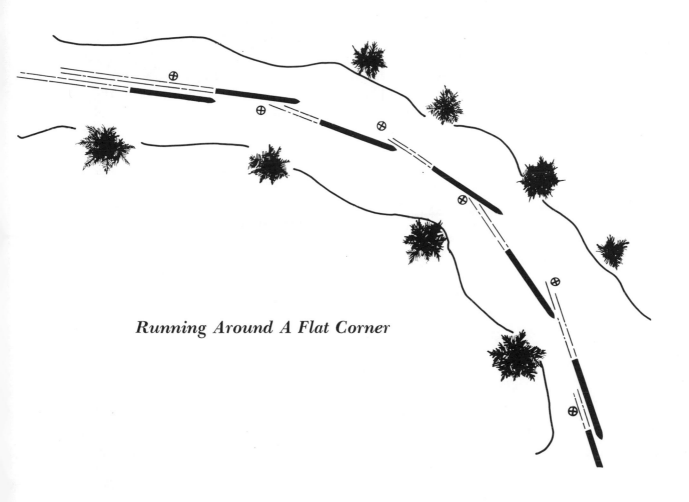

Running Around A Flat Corner

that, once the inside ski is placed in the new direction, you will have to hold with the corresponding pole while the outside ski, from which you are skate-stepping, is brought around and ahead with that pole going into action immediately as a power stroke. In reality you have effected a "change-up." The answer to the often-asked question whether the outside pole is used for holding prior to skate-stepping in the new direction depends on a number of factors: steepness of terrain, wax, initial velocity, etc.

Turning on the flat: Let us assume you are in the normal diagonal running position on flat terrain, where little or no holding is necessary to make the turn. In this situation, keep driving and simply ski around the corner step by step, turning slightly with each step but not breaking the rhythm of your diagonal technique. You will often see runners straighten up, lose their power, and walk around a corner. It costs them seconds on the turn and more still getting started again.

Running Bumps

On Uphill or Flat terrain, where little acceleration is possible beyond the velocity generated by your technique, your stride must be adjusted to the bumps so that you can kick off from *just over the top of the bump*. You must make the bumps work in your favor. Do not chance back-slipping by kicking off on the near side of the bump, when you can get a firm kick from just over the top; do not make your kick in the low spot between bumps. The key to running in rough terrain is the ability to stay loose in the hips, knees, and ankles, and to match your technique with the terrain. In many instances you will have to reach out in order to get the foot over the top of the next bump. You can take a longer stride by lowering the body and forcing the knees ahead.

Slight Downhill or Flat where acceleration is possible: The technique usually best suited to this terrain is the double-pole coupled with the

Running Bumps—Timing of stride must match the terrain

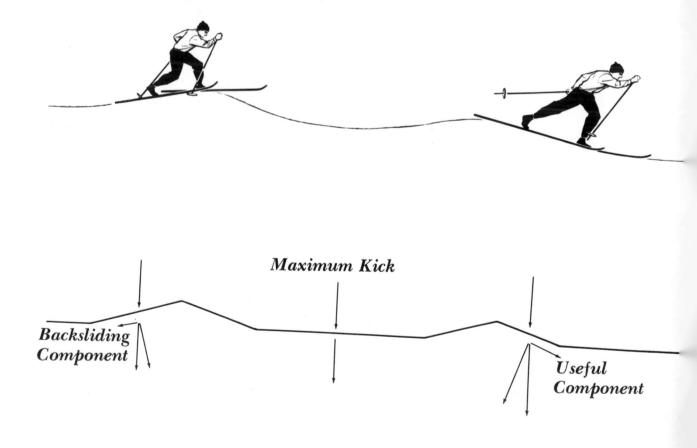

proper thrust of the knees and hips. Push downward on the downside of the bumps while continuing to double-pole. Here the flexibility and tracking qualities of the skis play a very important part: they must not only be flexible enough to track properly, but also stiff enough to spring you out of the bumps. Properly timed, this technique of running bumps literally shoots you ahead.

Where style and distance are the same thing...1960 Olympic champion Helmut Recknagel of Germany in action at Squaw Valley. His fine aerodynamic style shows exceptional stretch and finger-tip control of flight

Ski Jumping

Why do kids jump? Because they love it. Because it is the most beautiful thing they have ever done or are likely to do. Because, on a well-designed and well-conditioned hill, it is safe and easy to jump.

There is more fun in the sport for the all-round skier, and much to be learned from jumping whatever specialties the skier later follows.

Ski jumping is perhaps the most brief and intense of sporting events. Fifteen seconds pass between leaving the top of the inrun and the swing at the bottom; actual flight may last two or three seconds.

Jumping is a spectacular sport. It looks dangerous. Actually, however, jumping is quite safe, provided the hill is ready for jumping and the skier ready for a hill of that size.

There are hazards, of course, but they are not the ones usually imagined by worrying parents. They see speed, height, drop, but do not understand that, given good physical condition, a skier can handle such things with a flourish.

The Parts of a Ski Jump

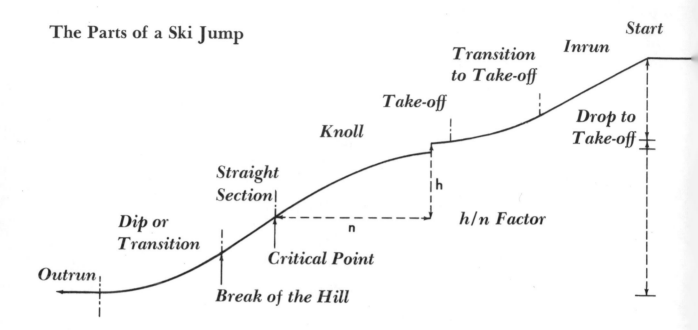

The most common hazards are:

1. Jumping on a big hill too soon.
2. Jumping on a hill not properly tramped out hard and smooth.
3. Jumping alone.
4. Jumping with the wrong kind of skis or boots.
5. Ice, ruts, glazy snow—especially on the take-off and in the dip of the landing.
6. Dogs and spectators.

Jumping skis are long and three-grooved and somewhat heavier than ordinary skis so they will "track" straight and ride on the air. Their stability and security, as compared to other skis, have to be experienced to be believed.

Children, however, need not start with jumping skis. It is better for them if they begin with their familiar downhill boots and downhill skis. The skis must be light enough to be manageable. Although it is good if jumping is started early—at the age of five or six—before alpine ski techniques become too firmly ingrained, the jump is not the place to learn how to ski.

148

Two things must be done to downhill equipment so that it will work for jumping:

1. Spare cable lugs should be placed forward under the toe plates and the cables released from their rear downpull positions.
2. Boots may be unlaced at the top hole or two. Sometimes placing a sponge-rubber pad under the heel will also help. The purpose of these changes is to allow sufficient forward flexion at the ankles.

This is absolutely necessary, for in flight the *lean from the ankles* is the most important single factor. And landings and take offs require the same freedom at the ankles. A stiff boot with a high top simply forces the skier over backward.

An inexpensive pair of downhill boots, with flexible soles but good uppers will often be ideal for young jumpers. (See Appendix: Equipment)

Note:
the range of motion at the ankles,
the limberness of the soles,
the position of the cable lugs,
the top holes unlaced,
the sponge rubber pads under the heels.

SHELDON VARNEY

Small-Hill Jumping

Jumping can only be learned on small hills where the speed, height, and shock of landing can be reduced to a minimum. You wouldn't expect a young diver to begin on a 10-foot board; neither should young jumpers start on anything larger than a 20-meter hill. Moreover the hills should be of proper trajectory design, for a hill which is too high and too flat, or a hill that pitches the skier out into space will establish a train of bad jumping habits and may permanently and needlessly scare a young jumper.

Two hills, side by side, one 15 to 20 meters, the other 30 to 40 meters, each with its proper speed, height, and trajectory curve, make an ideal setup for learning to jump, and a place where youngsters from age six to sixty can "train."

Jumpers must keep their own hills. It is necessary during practice and all too often during tournaments. But small hills are easy to maintain and by working on the hill the young jumper learns to connect the "look" of the hill with the "feel" of it, so that in time he will be able to estimate just what a hill will do to him and to make his jump accordingly.

1. Tramp out the landing whenever it needs it. Boot-tramp it first if it is soft, for a fall in soft snow is the quickest way to twist an ankle.
2. Always leave the hill well tramped out.
3. Don't jump in rain or hard thaw.

150

Ice, deep new snow, and *wet new snow* present special problems which are fully discussed in the Appendix. In any case, pay particular attention to the *condition of the take-off* and the *dip.* These are the danger areas.

Blue soap powder or *spruce boughs* alongside the take-off and dip are valuable guides to the jumper, especially in flat light or falling snow. A strip of bluing across the 'break of the hill' is also a great help in showing jumpers the limits to which they can stretch.

INRUN POSITION

Elementary Positions

This position will serve on a 90-meter hill; it can be learned on a 20. It is a very natural position, and a *restful* one, while at the same time offering a minimum of air resistance.

LANDING POSITIONS

HANSON CARROLL

The proper landing position at first seems a crazy tight-wire stance, but actually it is the easiest and safest way for coming out of the air.

Exercises using just the landing hill, dip, and outrun of your small jump may be of great help, for they remove all anxiety and allow you to concentrate fully on the feel of take off and landing positions.

1. Try running the landing hill in deep inrun and deep landing positions until your body learns the feel of them, until your skis run easily together, and your balance is not upset by the pressure in the dip.
2. Then try running over multiple bumps in both positions. If you are taut, the bumps will throw you; but if you can relax and let your skis flow over the bumps, you will be surprised how easy it is. That is the relaxed springiness of a good landing.
3. Lastly, practice both take offs and landings from a "looping take-off" (a short upshoot take-off) built on an absolute flat. A good looping take-off should send you up 4 to 6 feet in the air. There is no better practice for developing body control and a springy landing. The looping take-off should not be too abrupt at first, however, for it tends to throw you off your balance until you are used to the feel of it.

Perfecting the Take off

The take off extends from the time the jumper rises from his inrun position (chest still pressed against his knees), through the arm swing and jump, into the air and continues until he has attained his flight position. It is not a matter of just jumping hard on the lip. The purpose of the take off is to launch the jumper out over his skis where he can "get on the air" as quickly as possible. It is a forward rolling motion, ending in a snap timed to hit the lip of the jump. The proper take off is the same whatever the size of the hill. There is a fundamental physical problem here, however.

On a small hill: distance is largely the result of a sharp, strong jump.

On a big hill: distance is a matter of getting into an aerodynamic flight position as quickly as possible and riding the air as long as possible.

The dilemma here is due to the difference in wind pressure which is not a significant force at slow speeds, but which, on a big hill, is the controlling factor. The young jumper is likely to learn to jump straight up, and then jack over, rather than to roll out of his inrun position into a snap. Such a take off will give him good distance now, but will be wrong when he gets on a hill 40 meters or larger.

Concentrate on the lip of the jump, get your timing right. Jump so that your weight goes out over your tips, and, at the same time, flip your tips up so they will catch the wind pressure. Jump steady and *straight ahead;* if you twist in the air, you are probably trying too hard.

At this stage, *poise, timing,* and *a good lean from the ankles* are more valuable to you than distance.

And most important: *Do not fight your jump in an effort to place your hands on your hips.*

Let your arms move as your body calls on them to maintain balance. When your weight is out over your tips, your arms will come to rest easily and naturally in the air.

Omer Lacasse practicing on a 15-meter hill. This is an almost perfect landing. He has deliberately overjumped the hill, landing in the upper part of the dip, but no strain shows in his performance. Such a landing is the result of years of practice. It is so natural a habit now that the jumper never thinks of the landing. He is thinking instead of his flight, stretching it down to the limits of the hill, picking out his spot for landing. With a well-packed dip under him he knows there is no chance of falling.

Note:
the erect position of head, shoulders, body;
the weight carried more on the forward leg;

*Softening
the
Landing*

the complete spring action at hips, knees, ankles, feet;

the skis, solid on the snow;

the relaxation of the whole body.

The landing extends from the latter part of the flight, down through the transition of hill to the outrun. It is often called the "telemark position" but it is not a telemark and even less a "position." It is a complete rhythmic action designed to cushion the shock, catch the weight, and take the pressure of the dip.

A landing, of course, must begin in the air—at that point when you decide where you want to "put them down." You stop pulling for distance and straighten up your body. (Your arms come forward, your head and chest are raised in order to increase the drag of the wind so that you can straighten up). Straightening up like this is very important. Without it you will lose the spring action at the hips and leave your knees to absorb the whole shock.

Your tips are held a little up so that the limberness of the skis will absorb the first part of the shock of landing.

Then, as you take the snow, you shoot one leg ahead to catch your weight. At the same instant you let your *hips roll down,* and *under,* and *forward.* The action of the hips is like the turning of a cam on a camshaft, deflecting a straight shock into a smooth, easy motion.

And as part of the same motion you come back up part way, to the recovery position, to take the pressure of the dip.

Landings are the great watershed in learning to jump. It is the take off which controls your entire jump: grace in the air, courage, distance, are all determined by what you do on the take-off. But during the learning process it is largely the success in mastering a landing which decides whether you will ever be anything more than a mediocre performer.

Here are four youngsters in various stages of development jumping on an 18-meter hill:

1. Oops! A scared kid, doubling up his knees in the air, throws his tips down.
2. Landing from a moderate jackknife position. It is neither safe nor comfortable, as the jumper's tense body shows. He has not learned how to straighten up and let his hips roll down.
3. A pretty good landing after a long jump. He has no hill left under him but stands it easily. Body and knees are fine, arms natural. All he needs is to have his skis together under him.
4. Oops! Look out below. A caught inside edge and a sure fall. A game kid trying to jump with downhill skis and expensive downhill boots.

154

Typical American Landing?

It is fair to say that 75 per cent of the jumpers in this country never get beyond the beginning stages. Less than 10 per cent know what a good landing is. Not over 30 or 40 jumpers can make one. The trouble is that most jumpers, seeking the thrill of long jumps on big hills, never stop to learn a first-rate landing. They learn, instead, some makeshift method for getting down out of the air, and standing. It works. It becomes habit.

Such a landing will cost the skier 3 points in style (the equivalent of 30 feet in distance on a 60-meter hill) but he still feels that to return to a small jump for practice would be kid's stuff.

Things to remember

1. *Keep forward* "on them" as the Norwegians say. Don't sit back or pull back or back paddle. You can't make any landing with your weight back. If you are overjumping the hill, you still need your weight forward, for if you pull back then, the dip will take your skis right out from under you.

Here is a youngster learning the fundamentals well on a 10 m. hill. He soon wanted to jump "the big hill" (20 m.)

2. *Straighten up in the air.* If you land head down in a jackknife position, you have lost the spring action at the hips. You may pitch forward for a hard fall in the dip, or, overcompensating, you may flip back and fall.

3. *Skis together under you.* Even if you are not quite in balance over your skis, keep them together. A slight downhill turn after taking the snow will bring your skis under you. But spreading wide may mean a caught inside edge and a bad fall. (See item 6 previous page.)

In the air consciously straighten up the head and arch the shoulders as you approach your landing. On the snow, as you take your "split," consciously let your hips drop down and then *drive them forward.*

One point worth noting about a good landing is that, if an unexpected fall occurs, the jumper is down close to the snow where he will not get hurt. Were he standing up straight, or jacked over at the waist, he would fall like a tree.

157

Flight   A good jump is one beautiful motion from top to bottom; the flight is only the most apparent part. On big hills the jumper actually rides a curve of wind—much as a surfboarder rides down the crest of a Pacific roller. Men begin to get the feeling of catching the air on a 40-meter hill; from 60 meters up they ride it. Youngsters, being light, begin to catch the air on a 20-meter hill.

The judges, whose job it is to compare the jumper against an ideal standard, mark the whole jump from top to bottom but place more weight on the flight than on any other part. They watch for the four signs of a good jumper in the air: courage and quickness in leaving the take-off; a sense of drive out over the tips; poise and control in the air; quick adjustments to minor imperfections.

A good judge can determine not only a skier's skill and timing but also his state of mind by watching what he does in the air. If the jumper is inexperienced or frightened, there is no way he can hide it: his take off shows no zip; he hangs back in the air either standing straight up or doubling over in a horrendous jackknife; he lands any old way, feet apart, cowboy style.

Inevitably a jumper's landing shows in everything he does from the inrun down. If he has no confidence in what will happen to him when he hits, how can he lean out on his skis and pull for distance? How can he make a strong take off that will put him out there over the bottom of the hill?

Good preparation in the air, good landing, but held deep too long

FROM PÅ SKI

Here is a fine jump by a young Norwegian. It shows the skill and
confidence which result from good training. It shows the forward drive
of the body in the air, the easy carriage of the arms, the preparation
for landing. With more experience on larger hills this boy will be able to
ride even more forward over his skis, but for the time being his control
over the complicated actions of ski jumping is already excellent.

160

The take off controls the jump, but timing controls the take off. Timing, an instinct essential to all sports, can only be developed through much practice. In jumping you should work for timing first, strength of take off later; for nothing is more apt to make you jump too early or too late than trying to jump too hard.

Body positions in the air always reveal what happened on the take off:

1. *Jumping too early:* your tips tend to suck the take off, throwing your skis down in the air and your body forward.
2. *Jumping too late:*
   a. *On a small hill* you may jump with the heels of your skis still on the lip. This throws the tips way down, in danger of sticking in the knoll.
   b. *On a big hill,* the heels of your skis go down and you get your tips in your face.

Every jumper falls many many times. Through hard experience, he learns to fall without getting hurt. *The main thing is to avoid a twist, a roll, or somersault.*

1. You get both skis on the same side and hold them together, flat on their sides so they won't dig in and catch.
2. You get down flat on the snow and skid.
3. You relax "just like dead" with your arms out, holding your body in a skid.

The
Great
Illusion

Many jumpers suffer from a most pernicious illusion: the notion that the modern big-hill style, perfected by the Finns, consists of grabbing the buttocks in the air. Nothing could be further from the truth. The modern jumping technique is a matter of riding the air for all it is worth and reducing the drag of the wind to a minimum. The arms do not initiate an aerodynamic style; they have almost nothing to do with it. Their position—quietly carried at the side or straight ahead—is the result of that style.

Arms are essential to maintaining balance. Let them move naturally as your body needs them, until you have learned a forward lean such that they automatically become quiet in the air. Then holding them steady and ahead will help your forward drive. Only later, when you have the wind pressure of a 60- or 80-meter hill, will it be natural for you to hold your arms behind.

Big-Hill Jumping

Fads in jumping come and go, but style does not. Style shows a steady progression toward a recognizable and deliberate aerodynamic flight. The techniques of today differ only in subtle ways from the championship form of Sigmund Ruud and Reidar Andersen a quarter of a century ago. Yet the difference is important: modern jumpers understand wind pressure better; they use it by intent. Aerodynamics now determine what is good style.

There have been many good young jumpers in this country who showed remarkable "float." Paul Bietila and Ray Lambert were two who could ride the air to the dismay of their rivals. But it was not clear to them what they were doing. They could ride the air, but they did not know what riding it was.

Tulin Thams, the first Olympic champion, was the great pioneer. He broke with all former traditions and used a moderate jackknife style with good lean from the ankles. Tradition could not stand against such a jumper. Out went the swan-dive position, out went the dropping of the tips—just as lifting the knees in the air had gone out earlier.

Sigmund Ruud was the next innovator. He combined a quiet, graceful style with fabulous distance. Save for the slow swimming motions of his arms, Sigmund had an aerodynamic style fifteen years ahead of other jumpers.

Birger Ruud, the greatest jumper of them all, brought poise and control beyond anything anyone had seen in jumping. He knew wind pressure and used it craftily, but more to balance on than to ride upon, for Birger and those who followed him lost the lift of their skis by pushing the jackknife position to the peril point.

Then came the postwar Finns, Swiss, and East Germans, riding in a fashion which no one but wind-tunnel scientists had believed possible. On the giant hill at Oberstdorf, Tauno Luiro, a nineteen-year-old Finn, established the latest world record of 139 meters (456 feet). Dead a few years later of diabetes, Luiro in that short time had demonstrated beyond any doubt that *style and distance are the same thing*.

Fritz Tschannen, Jon Riisnaes, and George Thrane were the first to bring the new style to this country. Back home, Riisnaes, a Norwegian youngster, had been thought to have a "peculiar" style. Here, as a university freshman, he won every meet he entered, including most of the important Midwest tournaments. Jumping judges—trained in a former era—were skeptical. But the boy's poise in the air and his great float were not to be discounted.

Seventy
Years
of
Jumping

One judge, unusually candid, tells of his own enlightenment: "I'd heard about this Riisnaes kid, out West and all over. I wanted to see what he could do. But when he came off the take-off, he didn't seem to take any hop at all. Missed the take-off altogether, it looked like. I had him docked 2½ points right there. . . . But then I watched him and he kept going and kept going, and going, and going until I said, 'Yeesus, is this boy ever coming down?'

"So I said there may be something wrong with that take off, but I wish somebody told me how to make a mistake like that."

Aerodynamics

On a small hill distance is a function of spring on the take-off and on a big hill distance is a function of aerodynamic flight.

The change from small-hill to big-hill jumping comes between a 40-meter hill and a 60-meter hill—roughly between 35 m.p.h. and 50 m.p.h. The transition stages are necessarily confusing. For this reason the Finns say, "Do your early training on a small hill (for take offs and landings), and then go straight to a big hill and stay there."

Dr. Reinhard Straumann's wind-tunnel experiments in Switzerland have come close to defining what is the optimum-flight position. His findings have been amply proven by expert jumpers in the past ten years. They confirm the importance of having *a maximum lean from the ankles, very little jack at the waist, and skis riding up on the air.*

The skier doesn't actually fly. His body and skis combined do not present wing surface enough for that. The best he can achieve is a lift about like that of an ordinary airplane "mushing in." His position in the air is exactly that of a delta-wing jet taking off.

In recent years ski jumping has been dominated by Finnish and German jumpers. Old-style jumpers who fail to make full use of the air simply drop out on the hill 10 to 20 meters short.

Take off

The modern take off is not a jump in the usual sense. It has only one purpose: to get the skier "on the air" in the shortest possible time. The more the jumper has to rise up out of a crouch position, and the longer he stands straight, the more will be his drag. Drag means *slowing down.* So the jumper makes his take-off in a way which will preserve his flight speed.

The *old-style take off,* derived unmodified from small-hill jumping is a powerful "sats" at the lip of the take-off. The skier goes up and out. His skis meanwhile tend to drop at the tips from the power of the spring. The jumper has to work hard to get his tips up—then he can go on them and catch the air.

But it is a decisive moment! He has lost valuable flying speed.

The *modern jumper* never presents his extended body to the drag of

164

Einer Landvik's "Telemarkstyle"

Tulin Thams, 1924

Josef Henrikson at Holmenkollen

Peter Hugsted, 1946

Harry Glass, 1956

A short history of the development of the modern flight style.

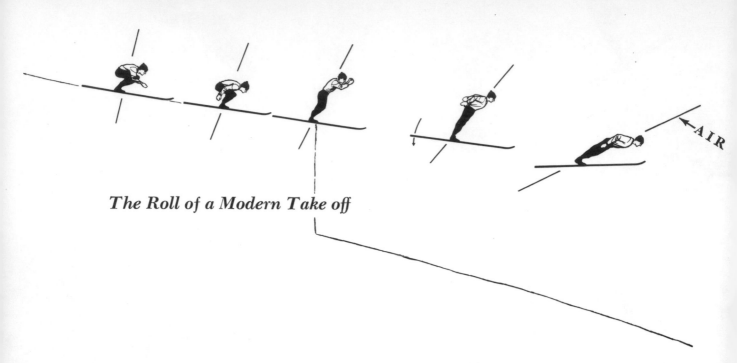

The Roll of a Modern Take off

the air. He rolls forward out of his crouch, timing his take off to be *just a little late.* The last straightening kick of the legs occurs in the air, which forces the heels of the skis down, the tips up, and the skier can go on them at once. The whole action may be completed and the skier in his flight position within 25 to 30 feet of the lip of the take-off.

The degree of arm swing on the take-off is by no means uniform. It follows the personal tastes and habits of the jumpers. Some, like the Russian jumper, Tskadse, use an extreme arm swing and one full rotation in the air. Some, like Kotlarek, use a moderate swing and rotation, quick and easy, like sea birds folding their wings in a dive. And others, like Karkinen, use almost no arm swing and no rotation at all, getting their full lean from the forward roll on the take-off. Therefore, it appears to make little difference which method is used, provided the swing of the arms does not increase the air-drag and delay the flight position.

The 1960 Olympic champion, Helmut Recknagel, of Germany, throws his arms backwards on the take-off, then straight forward in a full reach. From this extreme position he controls his lean, flight position, and preparation for landing simply by lowering or raising his finger tips!

Flight   Theoretically the ideal body position would be an airfoil curve, nose tip to ski tip, and elevated from the direction of flight by about 20°. But human factors must override theory. The skier has to control his flight. He must not cut through his wind pressure forward and tip over. And he must be able to straighten up for his landing. For this reason most big-hill jumpers favor a slight jack at the waist. It gives them an important margin of safety.

There is no way of separating flight from take off. They should not

166

be thought of as separate. Below is a sketch illustrating how the *air-drag is both greater and more prolonged in an old-style take off*. The skier loses precious flying speed and begins to drop. He is higher immediately after leaving the lip, owing to the strength of his jump, but his flight fades.

The modern jumper goes straight out. Low at first, he seems to gather speed over the hill and, in the end, rides higher.

The skier's body and his skis both contribute lift. In a sense they fly separately, joined only by loose bindings and loose boots and the common necessity of having to make a landing. It takes skill to hold the skis so perfectly together, yet it is a great safety factor, for if the skis drift apart, they move independently and may upset the jumper's balance. In addition when the skis are riding together, the total lift may be as much as 10 per cent more than when they are wide apart.

The effectiveness of a proper take off and an aerodynamic flight has not been a matter for debate since Luiro's spectacular showing on the Oberstdorf hill. At Squaw Valley, during the Invitational Meet in 1959, revealing data was obtained on speed and distance. A Straumann timer was placed on the take-off—two electric eyes 40 meters apart—

Old

vs.

New

Wind-Resistance Patterns

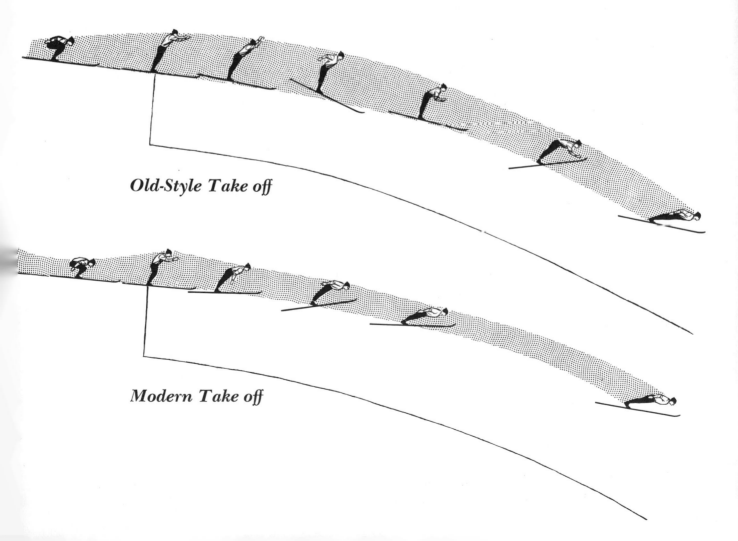

Old-Style Take off

Modern Take off

The beautiful rolling take off of Kalevi Karkinen, Finland.

in order to record inrun speeds. These speeds were compared to the distance marks, from which the following extreme example was taken.

Skier A was a well-known Olympic jumper from the Midwest, an expert in waxing, who, while he jumped strongly, failed to use the full lift of the air.

Skier B was Kalevi Karkinen of Finland, winner of the meet.

	SPEED ON TAKE-OFF	DISTANCE
A	57 m.p.h.	256 ft.
B	53.5 m.p.h.	290 ft.

Study these figures. They tell the whole story about the modern style in jumping.

World champion Juhanni Karkinen of Finland showing the perfect poise and relaxation of modern flight.

Whether the arms are carried behind or in a diving position ahead does not seem to make much difference. Both are aerodynamically sound. Dr. Straumann's wind-tunnel experiments seem to indicate that the jumper is more stable at high speeds if his arms are held behind, but the personal factor—what seems most natural to the jumper—is unquestionably more important than theory.

Big-hill jumpers have three ways of stabilizing their flight positions: the position of the arms, of the head and shoulders, and the angle of the skis. If the jumper is riding too far back on the air, he can double over farther, reduce the wind resistance, and force his tips down. If he is too far forward, in danger of tipping over, he can raise his head and shoulders, bring his arms up and out to the side, and let his tips come up. All three actions tend to rotate him back out of his perilous position.

Landing

Modern big-hill landings differ very slightly from those learned on small hills. The process of decision, straightening up, setting in, and recovery are all seen here. There is one important difference: *the landing action is half completed in the air.*

169

Flight and Landing

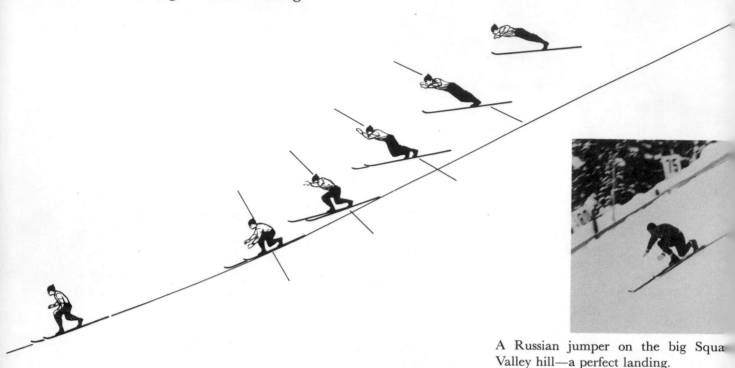

A Russian jumper on the big Squa[w] Valley hill—a perfect landing.

This is necessary because of the jumper's extreme forward lean. The jumper can straighten up his body, but he cannot pull back completely without loss of distance.

Instead, he does the following:
1. He relaxes his whole body.
2. He lets his tips ride up (from 20° to 30°), brings his arms to the side, shoulder height, raises his head and shoulders—all to increase wind pressure and help him straighten.
3. At the last moment of flight (because his feet are still behind him), he brings his knees and feet forward under him in the usual landing position—and then takes the snow.

The propriety of such a landing is debated among judges, some of whom feel it is "wrong" to start a landing in the air. It is wrong according to earlier concepts and rule books. Necessity will always be the final arbiter. With modern flight positions no other landing will do as well. The criteria should be safety, excellence in timing, and beauty of performance, not some outworn concept of what looks right or wrong.

Perfect timing is essential: if you split too soon, your skis separate —one up, one down—and your balance may be upset; if you split too late, you will not have your feet under you.

The giant hill in Oberstdorf, Germany, and the young
Finn, Tauno Luiro, who set the world's record of 456 ft.

Oh Lord, you made them so big and long-lasting, and I—I have so little time.

Appendices

Waxing
Equipment
On Running Ski Races
Training

Waxing for Recreational Skiing and Alpine Racing

Ski waxes have but one purpose: to reduce friction. For sixty centuries of skiing this problem has been approached in one way, namely, by trying to *waterproof* the bottoms of the skis. Only recently has it been clearly understood that *channeling air* under the skis is at least as important as the waxy substances used.

To the beginner, waxing has always seemed to be a mysterious, and rather sticky rite. Today, with a feeling of emancipation, the average skier has turned to the modern, plastic bottoms which, he is told, need no waxing.

At the outset, therefore, let us be clear on two points:
1. A fast ski is easiest to ski on.
2. All good alpine skiers, for all conditions of snow, use wax. They "paint" or "iron" their mixtures on hot and in "steps."

The beginner will recognize, of course, that there are two basic kinds of snow: wet snow and dry snow. With only two kinds of waxes —a wet-snow wax and a dry-snow wax—he can get along fairly well. Eventually, as his skiing improves, he will come to want the real freedom of a clean, fast ski; he will want to understand more about the drag between skis and snow and how best to overcome it.

A skier actually slides on a mixture of water and air. Just as the skater moves on a film of water under his blades, so the skier travels on water. Each point of ice is "greased" with water. In between is air. If this were not so, skiing on snow would be like skiing on sand.

When the weather is most favorable, a few degrees under freezing, and the snow has that fresh, fluffy quality, his skis will be fastest

173

because there are just enough ball bearings of water to let him slide easily and yet air enough in the snow to keep the total friction between water and skis to a minimum.

But let the snow be frozen hard, at ten below zero, and wind-blown into a compact mass, and his skis will be slow because of too little water, too little air, and too many harsh granular points scraping along them.

Or, on the other hand, let the weather warm up to sloppy, wet snow, and his skis will "suck" the surface because they are glued to the snow with a uniform, airless film of water.

Thus, the snow and weather introduce variables into the equation of friction:

Temperature is a factor because it controls the amount of melting that will occur as the ski passes over snow crystals. Snow gets slower and slower as the temperature drops. The necessary water to "grease" the projections of ice cannot form fast enough and that which does form grows more viscous with cold. Very cold snow, unless it is powdery, acts almost like sand.

Moisture content is important because it determines how much air there is between the crystals, how hard and smooth it will compact under pressure, and whether, with a rise in temperature, it will quickly compress into a glazed or wet surface. A simple test for moisture content in new-fallen snow is to take up a handful, squeeze it, and see whether it maintains its form or falls apart into powder again.

The *age* of the snow is also a factor of importance. Snow goes through many metamorphoses before the spring thaw. It begins its life in the familiar, vivid, six-sided crystalline form, complete with spicules and lacery. At once the changes start, the sharp points begin to evaporate, the star shapes become more plate-like and compact. Packing crushes them into conglomerations, wind smashes them, warm weather melts them into pellets of ice.

For waxing purposes three distinct crystalline states are commonly considered:

1. *New or fine grained snow* characterized by fine sharp-edged crystals.
2. *Coarse-grained crystals* characteristic of snow two or more days old. Upon being subject to cold weather the finer crystals adhere to one another becoming larger and more rounded.
3. *Crusted or corn snow*—characteristic of snow which has been subject to above-freezing temperatures and then refrozen, possibly many times.

Transformations of the state of snow may take days or weeks, or only hours. The soft hill, boot-tramped today, is still loose by evening, but in the morning will be solid enough for jumping or downhill. The powdery snow that blows from the turns like feathers now, after a few hours of wind will be breakable crust.

All of these considerations necessarily influence the selection of wax. No treatise could hope to present a fool-proof outline or chart of how to wax for all conditions. Waxing must remain a skilled operation to be learned by personal experience. The most that we can offer is a good standard of wax mixtures for standard conditions; it may serve as a basis from which more refined judgment can develop.

Stepping the Wax

Air is the latest discovery in ski waxes, perhaps the best of them all. For centuries all sorts of familiar substances were tried in an effort to waterproof skis: beeswax, rosin, pitch, pine tar, whale oil, camphor and many others. More recently there have been the synthetic waxes and resins, and the plastic bases. Only in the last ten or fifteen years have skiers learned the importance of putting on waxes in a way that channels air under the skis.

The principle is familiar enough. It is for the same reason that a fast hydroplane has steps under the hull. It is for the same reason that any speedboat will go faster in a light chop than on a glassy surface.

In skiing the introduction of air between skis and snow is accomplished in three ways:

1. Painting the wax on in steps. (This produces a number of fairly large, distinct steps.)
2. Ironing the wax on with a hot iron. (This produces a multitude of small ragged steps.)
3. Painting or ironing wavy lines in the wax. (The above, of course, refers only to treatment of the skis; one may also help accomplish the same result by packing or raking the snow, by throwing fresh corn snow over a wet inrun track, by freezing the snow with snow cement, etc.)

What the skier does is literally to shingle his skis with melted wax. He may paint only six or eight shingles on each side of the groove, or he may use as many as twenty-five or thirty, depending upon the speed at which he expects to ski and the characteristics of the snow. The wax may be hard or soft, the layers thin or thick, the strokes straight or wavy, or the top may be dressed afterwards with a hot iron. Only experience can determine what is likely to be the best mixture for a particular snow and how it should be applied.

175

A few general principles in painting on wax should be understood at the outset:

1. At temperatures above 20° F. use a relatively soft, water-repellent wax.

   Below 10° F. use a hard wax painted in thin layers.

   In between the waxes are mixed.

2. In wet granular snow which is quite abrasive, but where the suction of water is the main problem to be overcome, use numerous steps and relatively thick layers.

   In cold granular snow, which is highly abrasive because of the lack of water, use a thin, hard wax in few layers, or no wax at all.

3. Thickness or thinness is controlled in four ways: the number of layers, the heat of the wax, the rapidity of the strokes, and the thickness of the brush.

4. For anticipated high speed (downhill) use fewer steps, since each step has an inherent drag and since more air is present under the skis at higher speeds.

   For slower anticipated speeds (slalom) use many small steps, or iron on the wax.

5. Test your wax at the appropriate speed (not just on a gentle slope at the bottom) for a wax may feel fast at slow speeds but drag at downhill speeds, whereas other mixtures which feel a little slow at first may "take off" when the speed increases.

Painting for Recreational Skiing

The equipment is not costly, nor the application of the waxes difficult. The satisfaction of having good fast skis under you, you will find, is well worth the effort. You will not believe this until you have tried it, and tried it enough times to learn how to make it work.

Fit yourself out with:
A small pot with a cool handle (or clean tin can and pliers)
A thin 1¼ inch brush
A scraper
Steel wool and rag for cleaning skis
Swix Cake Binder—a "rub-on" binder for the wax
1 pound of white paraffin (canning paraffin)
2 cakes of Metro 8
2 cakes of Metro 9, or Swix Green, or Fall-line green
A source of heat—Sterno, Primus or kitchen stove.

Now for the snow. It requires no engineer's handbook, slide rule, or occult powers: simply take up a handful of snow, with a gloved hand, and squeeze it to see what happens.

	Mixture	Steps
If the snowball is wringing wet	paint on plain white paraffin	25
If the snowball is firm but not wet	½ Metro 8 ½ White paraffin	12–15
If the snowball falls apart	½ Metro 8 ½ Metro 9 (or similar wax)	7–10
In very icy conditions	use plastic or lacquer bare	

Binder

Since wax itself is a poor adhesive, a "binder" is commonly used which provides a tough, water-repellent, adhesive layer. Old-fashioned Skare, made of pine pitch and pine tar, used to be the universal binder, but its singularly black and sticky properties made it a menace to well-dressed skiers. Swix Grundvalla, the present favorite among racers, is a modern version with similar disadvantages. The Swix Cake Binder does not provide as good a bond for the wax, but for most purposes it is good enough, rubbed on thin and smoothed out with the hand or cork. Your wax job will *last much longer* if you take the time to put on a binding layer.

Application

Melt the equivalent of a 3 x 3 x ½-inch cake of wax in the pot. The brush, too, must be heated, but do not let the tips of the bristles touch the hot bottom of the pot. (Waxing should be done in a large airy room, or out of doors, for the fumes are noxious.) The skis meanwhile are warmed, cleaned, and the binder applied. When the wax begins to "smoke" it is nearly hot enough. Let it go a little longer. It must be hot, but not boiling.

Start painting, beginning at the heel of the ski and stroking forward, doing each side separately and covering the groove. Do not cover the entire steel edge; you will need the cutting edge bare.

Always wax in the groove. If you want to be able to turn extra easily at slow or moderate speeds, wax the grooves heavily.

If the wax runs out into streaks, often white because of air trapped under it, the wax is not hot enough or your ski is too cold.

The strokes should be about 18 inches long, which allows ample overlapping.

Paint the entire bottom and tip; at the shovel paint one stroke in the middle of the ski then two rapid ones on each side. If you want a really first-class job, paint the sides of the skis with a light coat as well.

Mistakes The most common mistakes are:

1. Wax not hot enough or the ski not sufficiently warm. The wax then cools and hardens too rapidly to be layered on smoothly; the steps may become too thick.
2. A bad brush, burned at the tip or gummy from use other than waxing.

Your skis are ready at once. Let the brush drain. Later, when the wax is cool, you may heat the can momentarily and knock out the remaining cake for future use.

Waxing is not difficult if you start simply and proceed in a methodical way. Start with the four mentioned basic waxes. Use them over and over in all kinds of snow and weather until you *know* what they will do. Record your findings.

The ultimate in waxing can be obtained by adding a few more specialty waxes. They should be added to your kit one at a time and only after extensive usage, both alone and in combinations with your basic waxes. No kit should have more than eight waxes. No mixture should contain more than three waxes.

Waxing for Alpine Racing

KIT

Grundvalla binder
White paraffin
Swix Red, Fall-line Red, or similar wax
Metro 5, 8, 9, 10, 48 (Olympia). Metro 1 or similar hard, tarry wax
Melting pot
Source of heat
Brushes 1½″ and ½″ (for sides of skis)
Small block of pine (to scrape wax from outside of steel edges)
Newspaper (for tying between tips and tails after wax job)
String
Cloth
Screw drivers (for bindings and edges)
Scraper
Steel wool
Knife (to have at the start in case of a bad guess on waxes)
Repair parts and screws
Bastard file for edges.

Air Temperature	Wax	No. of steps each side of groove	Thickness
35°–40°	½ Swix Red ½ White paraffin	20	thick
25°–35°	⅓ Metro 5 ⅓ Metro 8 ⅓ Swix Red	15	medium
15°–25°	½ Metro 8 ¼ Metro 5 ¼ Olympia 48	10	thin
5°–15°	½ Metro 8 ¼ Metro 9 ¼ Olympia 48	8–9	thin
–5°– 5°	½ Metro 1 (or similar hard wax) ½ Metro 9 (or Swix Green or Fall-line Green)	7–8	thin
Under – 5°	Metro 10	7	very thin
Wet Corn snow	⅓ Swix Red ⅓ Metro 5 ⅓ White paraffin	15	medium
Ice, harsh crust	no wax		
Sunshine and shade	wax for the slowest section		

Sharpening the Edges

Few skiers other than racers appreciate what a difference sharp edges make. With racers it may be more than just winning a race which is at stake; a serious crippling accident or even a fatal one could occur if the skis were not able to hold, on icy stretches or fall-away corners, the way the skier expected. With recreational skiers dull edges allow skis to perform at only a fraction of their true capabilities. Skiing with dull edges is about as sensible as driving a car with a flat tire.

It takes only a few minutes to sharpen edges. You need a vise for your skis and a "warding bastard" file (as distinguished from a "mill bastard"). The ski is set side up in the vise, with the bottom facing out, and the file is then laid across the top at about a 45° angle fore and aft. The offset of the edges allows the edge to be filed at a slightly acute angle as the bastard is laid just to clear the wood or plastic edge at the top of the ski.

File strokes are short, perhaps 6 to 8 inches long, and are made *longitudinally* rather than across the edge. Be careful not to rock the file down and roll or "burr" the edge, for this burr will change the gripping characteristics of the ski rather markedly. On ice the skis may suddenly grab and throw you. You probably would never think of racing on an untried pair of new skis; racing with freshly burred edges makes even less sense. The proper way is to keep your edges well honed and sharp at all times so that you know exactly what your skis are capable of doing, on hard pack or ice.

Waxing for Ski Jumping

"Shellac and paraffin" is still the universal formula for ski jumpers —the same combination for all snows. This old stand-by is good, but it may well be not good enough any more. The revolution which has taken place in alpine waxing during the past fifteen years has not yet been recognized by the jumping fraternity. Nevertheless, speed is what all this talk of waxing is about. And since there is no notable difference between downhill snow and jumping snow, downhill friction and jumping friction, since air under the skis is as important to one as to the other, it is probable that plastic bottoms and "stepped wax" will soon be found on the jumping skis of all top competitors.

The jumper is therefore advised to study with care the foregoing section on general waxing and waxing for alpine events. In particular when he is faced with high-friction conditions—cold wind-blown snow, or sloppy, wet snow—he should consider making the big switch to waxes and methods long since proved effective by the downhill skiers.

Yet there is something to be said for the lac and paraffin techniques. They are easy to understand, simple to apply. Any child can learn how to shellac the bottoms of his jumping skis and rub on paraffin to suit the snow. The child, the young jumper, the youngster jumping for his high-school team, should start with lac and paraffin and leave the more advanced alpine techniques until later.

Plain white shellac is good enough. It is the least expensive of the jumping lacs. It should be somewhat diluted with denatured alcohol and then, with a cloth, rubbed rapidly on a clean smooth ski. Four layers, with time to dry between, will produce a fine bottom. When it has hardened well, it may be further polished with fine steel wool until it shines like glass.

There are many commercial lacs which are made up specially for jumping and which are applied in the same way. They are not faster, but they do have the advantage of being somewhat tougher than shellac and so are perhaps a little better for children's skis.

Over this glassy surface, for most conditions, a thin layer of ordinary paraffin is rubbed. That is all. The amount of paraffin, and the way it is applied varies with different snow conditions, but these differences too are easily learned:

For cold old snow: thin paraffin polished with wool.
For very cold new snow: paraffin rubbed on in crosswise strokes. (To trap the air.) Do not polish.
For damp new snow or corn snow: rub on the paraffin rather thick and in a crosswise or rotational fashion. Leave rough.
For sloppy wet snow: paint on paraffin in 30 to 40 steps.

The above variations of the shellac and paraffin technique will serve well enough for the beginner and intermediate jumper. One word of warning: medium, and thick wax, as used in jumping is not to be compared to waxing for downhill. The youngster who starts in with downhill skiing and then tries jumping invariably rubs wax on too heavily. He will scrub a mass of paraffin over his jumping skis, even for cold snow, and then literally have to walk down the hill. Faced with wet snow, he will transform the bottom of his skis into a hopeless mess and then wonder why he gets no distance. The lac and paraffin technique must be used with discretion.

Another point is to be sure to *wax before trying the hill.* Especially in wet weather. Once the bare wood is wet, it is impossible to rub on a good layer of paraffin.

Waxing should be done on the sides of the skis as well as the bottoms and the grooves. Some people even paraffin the tops of the skis to keep them free from powdery accumulations of snow.

Waxing for Cross-Country Races and Touring

Cross-country waxes hold going uphill and slide going down. It seems like a miracle when you first run with well-waxed racing skis and find they will carry you up a 20° slope without herringboning and then run away from you on the downhill sections.

The reason for this performance is not so obscure as it may seem at first. Cross-country wax is always soft wax used fairly thick. When the weight of the runner presses the ski down against the snow, without sliding, the minute projections of ice can bite into the wax and hold. But when the ski begins to slide forward, friction melts the spicules of ice and the ski glides like a well-waxed downhill ski.

As stated earlier there are two basic types of snow: wet snow and dry snow. The beginner should start, therefore, with only two kinds of running waxes. They will do an 80-per-cent job for him under most conditions. Later he will find he needs other waxes for sloppy wet snow, moist new snow, crust, ice, wind-blown snow, new powder. He will discover that the thickness of the wax makes a great deal of difference in how it holds going uphill, and how long under adverse conditions it will stay on his skis. He will learn the importance of having a sticky, tough binder on the bottom of the skis, and how to mix the waxes by putting them on in layers and heating them into each other by the rubbing of his palms.

As he improves in his running techniques, strengthens his arms and shoulders and back, the beginner will find that a fast ski with relatively less climb is preferable to a slower ski with good climb.

He will learn that races are won by waxing as much as by technique or brute strength. With good wax—and in spite of everything others have told him—he may discover he loves cross-country racing.

Whether he races or not, he may find that the knowledge of how to run, the kind of equipment to use, and the way to wax, will bring him unimagined pleasures later on in ski mountaineering or easygoing touring.

Cross-country waxes are classified as to their hardness or softness. The soft waxes are called klisters:

1. Skare Klisters—for coarse, frozen crystals below freezing temperatures. The so-called harsh condition.
2. Tor Klister—for above-freezing conditions; both new wet snow or wet corn snow.

The hard waxes are commonly classified according to a color or number system which simply indicates the degree of hardness. For example: Swix uses a color system of green, blue, purple, and red; Rex uses green, blue, red, and yellow; Kiva, on the other hand, uses numbers one, two, three, four, five, and six.

Before surface waxing the racer should first ensure that the skis are well prepared for waxing.

Base Waxing

The so-called base wax or ground wax, performs several important functions:

1. to preserve the bottom of the ski against wear,
2. to act as an adhesive for the surface waxes, and
3. to waterproof the bottom of the ski.

Cross-country skis do not have plastic bottoms as do our downhill, slalom, and jumping skis, so especially good care must be taken of the running surface. Many of our top quality racing skis are made of birchwood, which is not tough in respect to its resistance to harsh, crusty, or

182

SWIX CROSS-COUNTRY WAX CHART

Snow Characteristics

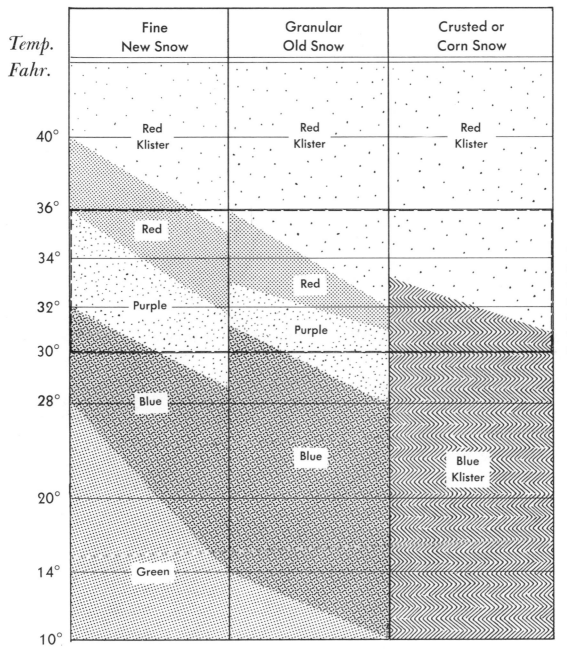

Temp. Fahr.	Fine New Snow	Granular Old Snow	Crusted or Corn Snow
40°	Red Klister	Red Klister	Red Klister
36°			
34°	Red		
32°	Purple	Red	
30°		Purple	
28°	Blue		
20°		Blue	Blue Klister
14°	Green		
10°			

This is the trouble-some temperature range.

Moisture

Start by waxing for the coldest conditions you expect to encounter. The "drier" the snow the higher your cold snow wax will work.

icy conditions. New skis should be scraped and sandpapered, if the bottoms are covered with an oily coating, and impregnated with pine tar burned in with a torch. Some advocate a mixture of pine tar and linseed oil. The oil, being a drying oil, adds a protective layer around the wood fibers, greatly increasing their toughness. When the skis will not take in any more tar, wipe off the excess, leaving the bottoms practically dry.

In many instances it is desirable to have an adhesive on the bottom of the ski to aid in holding the surface wax. A very thin layer of pine tar (burned on and wiped off, or corked on) will serve this purpose, although there are special "ground waxes" that are far superior to pine tar for this purpose. Ground waxes should be very thin—a few molecules thick is enough to provide a bond between wood and the surface waxes. "Enough to make a thumbprint" is an old standard to go by. If thicker than that, the ground wax may work up into the surface layers and cause slipping, or icing of your running wax, especially when the latter is thin, or in those tricky conditions that hover around 32° F.

Owing to pressure and friction, there is always a certain degree of melting of the snow crystals which are in contact with the ski. Though present in minute quantities a majority of the time, the moisture may become excessive. The wax itself must therefore be impervious to water —"unwettable"—and it must further prevent moisture from reaching the wood fibers.

Studying the Snow Conditions

Before considering the surface waxing, a very careful survey should be made of the immediate conditions. Check the air temperature, moisture content of the snow, and the type of snow, according to the principles outlined earlier.

Keep track of the long-range weather forecasts so you will know of the approach of warm and cold fronts. A new front may move in within the hour preceding a race. Or, worse, the snow may change radically during the course of a race. You must be able to anticipate such changes and plan your waxes accordingly.

Trial Waxing

Once the initial survey of both the existing and forecast conditions has been made, it is time to experiment. The reader may wonder why we do not simply refer to some convenient wax chart and let it go at that. There is a very good reason: you can't wax "by the book." Experience has proven time and time again that there are too many variables to be covered in any one chart.

Three ancient rules of waxing will serve you in good stead. Memorize them:

1. *Wax for the hardest (harshest) conditions you expect to encounter.* For ice you will need the hard klisters (Skare); they are tough and will last. If there is new or fine-grained snow blown into the track, you may have to apply several layers of a fine-grained snow wax over a layer of hard klister. Should you wax just for the fine-grained snow, the ice will soon scrape your skis bare.

2. *Wax for the coldest conditions you expect to encounter.* The hard waxes will usually work to some extent even though warmer conditions should be encountered. A melting snow wax, however, will usually ice up the minute colder conditions are encountered. Start with the coldest combination of waxes you think will serve and work toward the warmer until you find the wax that gives you the best combination of speed and kick.

3. *Wax for speed first, then as need be, add for kick.*

Waxes: There are many fine brands of wax available today. It is not our intent to advocate one kind more than the other; most of them on the market are good. Whatever you do, *learn one brand well* at the start. Do not try more than one brand until you understand that one thoroughly. Learn the strong points and weaknesses of each wax in your set. Keep experimenting with them; keep records. Once the weaknesses have been identified in one brand, then set out to find reinforcements from among the other makes of waxes. The man who carries three or four different brands in his kit is a confused waxer.

Applying Wax

The "surface," or "running," waxes are applied in layers. Unless the waxes are going to be blended, smooth out each layer individually. It is better and quicker to do this than to apply gobs of the wax and struggle to smooth them out. Whether the layers are all of one kind, as outlined in the wax chart, or blends of two or three waxes, will depend upon the actual conditions which you are testing. These wax layers may be smoothed out by ironing, corking, or simply rubbing with the hand. (Some modern waxes are changed by a hot iron, so check the directions carefully.) Corking is undoubtedly the most acceptable method; ironing will give a harder, faster surface; rubbing with the palms gives a wax job that will be slower but have a better grip for climbing. Should the air temperature be at the lower temperature range of the wax under consideration, try ironing first; then if the skis slip backward, try ironing the first layer and corking the second layer. Should you be using Swix Blue hard wax on an old snow track with the temperature between 15° and 25° F., try ironing; if from 25° — 30°, try corking; and if around 32°, try just rubbing the wax in with the gloved hand. Many times you can get by with a colder snow wax in a warmer temperature range by rubbing instead of corking.

Klister waxes are best put on at room temperatures after both the wax and skis have been allowed time to warm up to room temperature. Direct heat may be used as an aid in smoothing out some waxes; with others heat will destroy their usefulness.

Cross-country waxes must often be mixed, or blended, in much the same manner as downhill waxes. The only difference is that instead of melting the waxes in a pot and painting them on (as in alpine waxing), the waxes are rubbed directly on the ski and then blended by palm or iron. As an example, assume the temperature is close to 32° F. and Swix Blue has started to slip, but you do not wish to go to Purple: rub on a medium layer of Blue, then a thin layer of Red, and iron them together. You have now blended ⅔ Blue with ⅓ Red. It may be necessary to repeat this process in order to get a second layer.

Testing the Wax

Once applied, the wax should be allowed to cool and then skied on for some minutes before an accurate judgment can be made of its sliding and climbing qualities. Too many racers test their wax by taking a couple of short turns in a nearby patch of snow and then, smitten with race fever, start complaining, or fiddling for some lucky magic combination. The wax has to have a chance to adjust to the crystalline structure of the snow.

Wax for speed first; then as you try your skis and wear in your waxes, if you find you do not have enough kick, it is very easy to apply a small amount of softer wax under the foot and cork it on. It is also very important that the skis be tested on a track similar to that on which you will be racing. The track must be firm so you can really bear down and kick. An honest appraisal cannot be made on a soft track.

Waxing on the course during a race is permitted as long as it is done by the racer himself. Should there ever be doubt about the course and the wax, carry a tube with you. If your estimates go wrong, then kick off your skis and change the wax job immediately; many minutes may be saved in the end. In any case, *always carry a small flat scraper and some paraffin in your pocket.*

Remember, the best of Olympic racers sometimes misguess the weather and are fooled about the wax. The foregoing principles of waxing are not guaranteed to keep you out of trouble. But they will usually do so. They will serve as guides until a "waxing instinct," refined by much experience, serves you better.

186

Equipment for Recreational Skiing and Alpine Racing

The beginner walking into a ski shop for the first time is due for a shock. There stands a stack of blue and red and black skis more beautiful than Stradivarii—and almost as expensive. There are boots as big as cement blocks—$35 to $80. There are the stretchies, sweaters, parkas, gloves, goggles, which look so swell on Stein Eriksen. . . .

At this point, the beginner is likely to wonder whether he has mistaken bankruptcy for a sport.

Skiing can be expensive, it can be a lifelong addiction to spending money, but it doesn't have to be. The person whose requirements are modest, who wants little more than to be able to hike his favorite hills and trails in winter, can choose simple boots and touring skis and be set for five or ten years.

If his ambitions are toward downhill skiing, he must accept the cost of the ski-lift culture. Nevertheless the prices need not come as high as the first tags say. Skis actually range (in 1960) from $15 to $150, and boots from $10 up.

The beginner should keep in mind two facts:
1. *Good boots are more important than good skis.*
2. *Short skis are easiest to learn on.*

With good boots a person can manage almost any skis. But not even a Toni Sailer could ski on his one-hundred-dollar skis if shod in basketball shoes. Boots are the skier's ultimate connection to the sport. With good skiers they become a joint of the body. The minimum one should pay for downhill boots is $25; those in the price range of $35 to $50 may well be worth the difference. Properly cared for, good boots will last three to five years, or even longer.

Boots

A *high-fitting double boot* is essential for anyone who will be doing mainly downhill skiing. The sole should be quite inflexible; and it should be narrow so as to permit the skier to bring his skis tightly together. Metal sole protectors on heel and tip are desirable.

The *inner boot* is of light leather, like that of a good gym shoe. It is designed to conform to the shape of the foot and to hold the foot firmly down against the sole. It should be of good workmanship, well stitched and strong, but not rigid.

The *outer boot* is to give support. It needs to be of heavy leather, tanned hard and polished smooth. Good leather, and good workmanship in making a boot strong enough to withstand the rigors of skiing,

187

are what make the price high. An examination of the quality of the leather alone is enough to tell you whether the boot is likely to be good.

When trying on a new boot, lace the top securely so that your heel will be forced back into the very cup of the heel. When this is done, the toes should nearly—but not quite—touch the front of the boot.

A new boot will always seem tight. The skier will have a hard time deciding whether the boot will cause painful pressures at certain points or will "work in" to fit the foot precisely. No one can tell the skier more than his own feet will tell him.

On the other hand, it can be said without reservation that *if a new boot feels entirely comfortable the first time worn, it will be too loose* after a few weeks of skiing.

If the boots are made of stiff, well-formed leather, lace both the inner and outer boots less tightly, thus preserving circulation and warmth. (*Exceptions:* Jumping boots and cross-country boots, which will be mentioned separately.)

There is one other kind of boot which should be mentioned here —that is one which a beginner would want if his desires are for general recreational skiing, with a fair amount of touring and easy going mixed in with some downhill running. Here a combination must be found which allows the flexibility for walking and touring and yet has the stiffness necessary for downhill running. While it sounds like an impossible compromise, such is not the case. An inexpensive downhill boot—say of the range of $15 to $20, and made of good leather—may have flexibility in the sole but enough stiffness in the uppers to do the job. With a simple touring hitch forward and a separate downpull hitch behind, this combination can be quite satisfactory. It is essential, however that the sole, though flexible, be tough enough to stand the tension of the downhill attachment without buckling at the instep.

Socks

The number of socks means very little to the warmth of the foot; that is more a matter of maintaining circulation in the toes and keeping away moisture. One can wear boots without socks, or with as many as four pair. As a compromise try two thin pair of wool socks.

Be sure, when you put the boot on, that the foot is dry. Do not remain very long in a warm room, for perspiration will later make the feet cold.

Skis

If all the skis in the world were laid end to end, they still would never satisfy man's desire for choices. Slalom skis, downhill skis, giant slalom skis, combos, glass skis, metal skis—when will there be enough alternatives? When will skis be good enough?

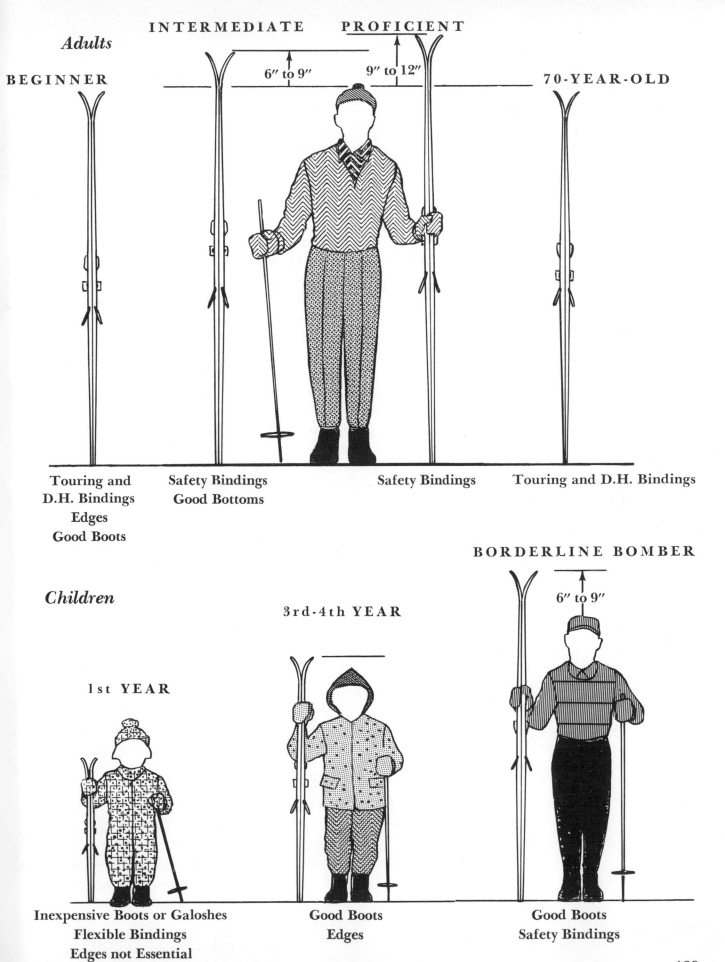

Adults

BEGINNER   INTERMEDIATE   PROFICIENT   70-YEAR-OLD

6″ to 9″   9″ to 12″

Touring and
D.H. Bindings
Edges
Good Boots

Safety Bindings
Good Bottoms

Safety Bindings

Touring and D.H. Bindings

Children

BORDERLINE BOMBER

6″ to 9″

3rd-4th YEAR

1st YEAR

Inexpensive Boots or Galoshes
Flexible Bindings
Edges not Essential

Good Boots
Edges

Good Boots
Safety Bindings

189

Emphatically never.

No book written after 1930 could hope to describe all the varieties of skis available to the buyer. We will not try. The racer knows from experience what he wants; the intermediate skier tends to follow the racer even when he should not; and the beginner simply doesn't know what he wants.

Beginners, children and older people should go to short skis, starting with inexpensive, one-season throwaways whose length equals their own height.

Let no suave store clerk sell you on something that "will last you several years." This is a delusion. If they are good for several years, they are too long and heavy to learn on. They are, in truth, an invitation to slow progress, frustration, and perhaps a plaster-cast vacation.

Better a season or two on short skis; then when you've learned the fundamentals of skiing and are in control, having fun, you can let yourself consider a longer better ski.

Young children will learn to ski in a matter of days if their skis reach only to their shoulders. But put them on skis as high as a "bent-arm reach" and they'll struggle a few hours and then go back to the television. Children are like adults, only smarter. They recognize that when a sport is no fun, it's no sport.

In skis you look at length, weight, edges, springiness, shape when bowed and pressed together, camber, running surface and finish. You also look down the running surface lengthwise to make sure that there is no *twisting* or *lateral warping*.

Prices range from $15 up, and an inexpensive ski may be just what you want. The *finish* may guarantee excellent workmanship or it may hide poor wood. In any case the modern high-polish finish or plastic covering would be justified as necessary for keeping out water. Wet wood, allowed to dry, checks and cracks and rapidly goes to pieces.

Ski design is no mystique. Modern skis are wonders of wood engineering.

Here are a few principles that may help in the selection of a good ski.
1. The faster the speed the longer the ski needs to be.
2. For ice and hard snow a stiffer ski will hold better than a limber ski.
3. For bumps, moguls, and soft snow a limber ski will be easier to handle than a stiff ski.
4. Wet snow glued to wet wood by means of water produces the greatest drag. There are good lacquer and plastic bottoms *which don't wet,* and many of varieties of waxes. They should be considered as much a part of your skis as the wood itself.

Nowadays metal skis are coming into vogue. They are popular because they require no care, no waxing (it is believed), and because they "turn easy." Such skis are especially suited to the average recreational skier, for they seem to turn almost with the wish. But they can be tricky on hard snow, and at high speeds they do not track very well. Racing models, of course, will soon be perfected. But for the rank beginner, a moderately soft short pair of wood skis will serve him best in his first year or two.

Modern safety bindings have been developed to a point where it is unreasonable to ski without them.

Bindings

There are many kinds of safety bindings on the market. They all work on the principle that, if the pressure of the foot is straight ahead and not abnormally great, the ski will stay attached, but if an unusual twist or strain should come, the bindings will release. Some bindings release only with lateral or twisting strain. Some release if the pressure forward or backward, as in a forward fall, or backward fall, becomes excessive. Some release only at the toe, others release at both toe and heel. *And none is worth a nickel if not carefully adjusted and kept in adjustment.*

The beginner, in selecting a safety binding, should take the time to study its mechanism: What is it designed to do, and what is it designed not to do? Only if he thoroughly understands the binding can he adjust it to suit his foot, his weight, and his way of skiing. In general the wider range of conditions under which the binding will release, the safer. That is to say a safety binding which will open only at the toe is not as good as one which opens with pressure at both toe and heel. Or a binding which only releases under conditions of twisting strain is not as good as one which will take care of a straight over-the-tips fall as well. But additional functions require additional mechanisms and more complicated adjustment.

There are some exceptions to the use of the safety binding:
1. They are not good for jumping.
2. Most of them are not suitable for touring or walking.
3. Children, at least small children, do not have the weight to effectively release the bindings, or the comprehension to keep them in proper adjustment. (In this case a short ski is the best substitute for safety binding.)

The question of where the foot and the binding should be placed on the ski will always be subject to individual preference. But for the ordinary skier this simple rule will do pretty well:
1. The length of the ski (as measured from tip to heel along the running surface, including the curve of the tip) is divided exactly in half and a line drawn across the top of the ski at this point.
2. The toe of the sole (if European size 42) is placed exactly at this line and the binding mounted.

*Placing
the
Binding
on the Ski*

3. For each full European size, larger or smaller, the toe of the boot is shifted forward or backward, respectively, ½ cm. from this line. (That is: if the boot is European size 43, then the toe of the boot is placed ½ cm. forward of the line; or size 40, 1 cm. behind the line.)
4. The center line of the foot should be exactly over the center line of the ski.

Long Thongs, Check Straps, etc.

There is no hazard, on commercial ski slopes, quite so unpardonable as a runaway ski. Many a skier—including many a child—has been injured by skis traveling loose down a slope, coming like a hurled javelin. The use of safety bindings, therefore, places a special obligation upon the skier to make sure that his skis will not run away from him in a fall.

Some commercial operators will not allow skiers to use their tows without provision against this danger: either through the use of long-thong and Arlberg straps, or by the smaller check straps. Probably the long-thong and Arlberg straps are the best, for they help hold the skier's foot firmly down in his boot as well as providing a link between the skier and his skis, whereas the check straps, clipping on rings or laces, often become ripped or broken in a bad fall.

There is one hazard which the user of a safety binding must accept. That is the possibility of being himself hit—often on the head—by his own ski which, released in a fall but tied to his foot, may flail through the air and smite him mightily. There is no way to avoid this danger and yet have the measure of safety provided for by the binding. When one hazard is weighed against the other, it must generally be conceded that a safety binding, properly adjusted, is a worth-while investment.

Poles

Ski poles may be made of cane, metal, or fiber glass. The length is a debatable point among experts, but in general the skier will do well with poles which (while he stands on the ground or floor, not the snow) reach up to his armpits.

The straps at the top of the poles should not be too long or loose; that is, the skier's gloved hand should rest about 1 to 1½ inches below the top of the pole when the latter is grasped firmly.

The rings at the bottom—baskets, as they are sometimes called—should be small and light. Big rings are clumsy to manage and do not give enough added support in deep snow to be worth the extra weight.

Clothing

Here is a mess! Skiing has changed from being exclusively a "sport" indulged in by hardy men and women to being "fashionable." That is to say fashion has invaded the sport, bringing with it all the paraphernalia of changing styles, fashion shows, advertising gimmicks, marketing psychologists, public relations poets, etc.

"Buyer beware" was a slogan old in the days of Rome. The authors must beg to be relieved of the task of advising any potential buyer on how to look chic in ski clothes. There are plenty of others paid to give such expensive advice.

On the other hand clothes are important: first, for warmth; second, for freedom of movement; third, because a skier who looks good in well-fitting ski clothes is that much more in a mood to *look good* on skis, to ski precisely and expertly.

There is no question but the modern elastic stretch pants fulfill a function that is more than just aesthetic. They are ideal ski pants, being made of excellent material, having elasticity where freedom of movement requires it, and helping to make a skier want to ski at least as well as his pants look. Knickers, also, are good. They give somewhat more freedom of movement. For ski mountaineering and touring stretch pants are not recommended. Here something tough and baggy is desirable.

Ski sweaters and parkas, in the same way, fulfill a function of glamorizing the wearer, but this does not detract from their importance in keeping the skier warm. It should be said further, that no skier should attempt more than practice-slope skiing—no touring and high mountain work—without making provision for icy winds and driving snow. One heavy sweater or a couple of light sweaters, and a wind-break parka, are necessities.

Gloves

In general the better looking the handwear may be, the more cool it will be. Most fancy gloves are worthless in temperatures below freezing. The skier should wear a rather loose glove which has a wool lining. In cold weather, in temperatures down to zero or below, only a loose leather mitten with wool liner will keep the hand and fingers warm.

Racers, of course, wear thin, skin-tight leather gloves with knuckle protectors. Their fingers may be cold, but for the few moments of the race their poles are part of them.

A wool cap and a hood to the parka are desirable as safety against sudden bad moods of weather. Sunglasses to protect the eyes from glare on bright days and a sunburn preventive should be in every skier's kit.

Other Items

Goggles are often helpful, especially when it is snowing. Not only do they prevent snow from getting in the eyes, but, if the glass is of an amber or orange color, it helps resolve the flat light into the subtler shades which reveal bumps and hollows, ice and ruts. With interchangeable celluloid shields one may have amber for flat light; pale blue, green, or gray for bright sun; and clear for ordinary conditions.

Though racing equipment is constantly being changed and perfected, as of 1960 these items appear to have general approval:

BOOTS: Use only fine, narrow, double boots, allowing, when well broken in, forward bending at the ankles.

BINDINGS: Long-thong bindings with a turntable attachment and heel spring to increase forward tension on the boot. Used in conjunction with a good toe-release unit.

There is one exception: In racing slalom, the safety binding should be put into the non-release position, or the conventional binding should be used. In training, however, for all events the safety devices should be working.

POLES: Strong light cane for slalom, steel for downhill, small baskets.

SKIS: The finest wooden racing skis with Kofix or Celolix plastic bottoms. (Unless finer metal skis and better bases are perfected in the future.)

When skis are pressed together, you should not see light between them at any point. Nor should they be able to rock on each other, owing to convex surfaces at the tips. They should be flat or even slightly concave laterally.

Good racing skis are heavier and stiffer than ordinary skis. They have to be to hang on hard snow or ice on fall-away turns and to track properly over bumps at the speeds required in racing.

Racing skis are not satisfactory for "slope doping," *i.e.,* hopping and jumping in a leisurely fashion down moguls. They were not designed for such work and should not be so used. (This is a warning to the recreational skier: do not try to use racing skis unless you intend to employ racing techniques at racing speeds.)

EDGES: Interlocking, tempered, offset edges are essential, made of a steel which can be sharpened. The most recent innovation in racing paraphernalia are the so-called "hidden edges," which are covered by a plastic running surface on all but the outer 2 millimeters of cutting edge.

(Examine the edges closely. If the screws look neat and even, the holes were bored too large. But if the screws have had to be filed, they were probably set in hard.)

PANTS: Racing tights or stretch pants or ordinary pants tied below the knee.

CRASH HELMET: for downhill.

GOGGLES.

GLOVES: Thin and tight-fitting in order to feel the poles well.

WARM MITTENS, WARM-UP PANTS, JACKET: To be discarded just before the start.

Specifications for Racing Skis

SLALOM COMPETITION SKIS

LENGTH

If you are 150 lbs. weight—try 210 cm.
　　If you are 175 lbs. weight—try 215 cm.

WIDTH

Narrower than downhill skis—3 to 5 mm. at all points. Example for:
210　　　87 mm. at tip, 70 (waist), 78 tail.
215　　　89 mm. at tip, 72 (waist), 80 tail.

FLEXIBILITY

For holding and rapid turning, the ski should be relatively stiff in the middle third and slightly softer in the tip and heel. (The bend is bow-shaped but strong. Do not confuse a weak section of wood with what is meant by being "slightly softer.")

EDGES

Interlocking tempered steel 6–7 mm. wide and offset about ½ mm.

BINDINGS

Conventional. Or safety screwed down so as not to release. The bindings may be offset toward the inside, that is, so the center line of the foot is shifted ¼ to ½ cm. to the inside of the center line of the ski. (This gives better leverage on inside edges and helps in running hard courses.)

CAMBER

4 cm. which can be pressed out only with a firm squeeze.

DOWNHILL COMPETITION SKIS

LENGTH

220 cm. for average size skiers.

WIDTH

Wider than slalom skis—3 to 5 mm. at all points. Example: 92 mm. (tip), 75 (waist), 83 (tail).

WAIST

Thicker, heavier than slalom skis.

FLEXIBILITY

An *even bend* throughout its length except for a slightly softer tip. (The general arc-shaped curve of the ski when under pressure is designed to carve a high-speed racing turn with minimum skidding.)

EDGES

"Hidden edges."

Place the toe of the boot slightly back of the normal position (as discussed in recreational equipment). Foot is centered.

CAMBER

2 cm. of firm camber.

GIANT SLALOM SKIS

LENGTH

215 cm. for average-size skiers. These skis are more like downhill skis than slalom skis.

WIDTH

Example: 89 mm. (tip), 73 mm. (waist), 80 mm. (tail).

EDGES

Normal edges. "Hidden edges" for soft courses.

FLEXIBILITY

Even bend throughout except for tip which should be quite soft. (The soft tip is to cushion the shock of multiple sharp bumps.)

BINDING PLACEMENT

Normal position fore and aft and normally centered.

CAMBER

3 cm. of firm camber.

Equipment for Jumping

Jumping is an airborne sport, straight down the fall-line. There is little turning to be done except at the very end. For this reason jumping skis are longer and heavier than ordinary skis and have three grooves down the running surface.

The first thing a skier discovers, trying jumping skis, is the remarkable sense of steadiness and security they give him. The loose bindings seem strange for a while to one trained in downhill skiing. Take-offs, flight, and landings are quite different from those of downhill. Jumping, however, is a different sport, requiring not only different equipment but a mind and body unencumbered by downhill habits. That is why jumping should be begun early.

There are four guiding principles in the selection of equipment:
1. Young children (five to ten years old) should start jumping on their regular downhill skis.

2. Jumping skis should be heavy enough to be steady but not too heavy to manage.

3. Warped or twisted skis are dangerous. Don't sell them or give them away in a fit of kindness—saw them up.

4. Bindings and boots must be flexible, allowing a full range of motion forward.

Most young children love jumping and learn it very quickly. For the first season or two they will be better off with their familiar downhill skis and downhill boots. When they have begun to make jumps of 30 or 40 feet, showing steadiness and the rudiments of a proper landing (and when they have the strength to manage the bigger skis!), it will be time to think about special jumping skis. *Skis*

Two things need to be done to downhill equipment to make it suitable for jumping:

1. Place a separate pair of "cable lugs" forward under the middle of the toe plate, releasing the cable from the usual lugs.

2. Boots should be unlaced at the top, if necessary, to allow free forward flexion of the ankle.

It is difficult to find children's jumping skis. American manufacturers make no jumping skis less than 7 feet in length—unsuitable for a child under twelve or thirteen. Nevertheless perfectly good small jumping skis can be made from medium-sized downhill skis, provided they have no plastic base or edges and are not too stiff or heavy. Two more grooves are cut in the bottoms, one on either side of the central groove, with a mechanical router. With reasonable care such small jumping skis will last ten or fifteen years and be serviceable for many potential big-hill riders.

"As high as you can reach and a little bit higher," is the old saying, and good enough for the average ski jumper. High-school and college-age jumpers will want to add about 4 inches to their full-arm reach; big-hill jumpers use skis even longer—running from 8 feet to 8 feet 5 inches. *Length of Jumping Skis*

Skis that are too light tend to "swim;" those that are too heavy run away with you. It used to be thought that jumping skis were only long stiff planks. Weights up to 18 or 19 lbs. per pair were not uncommon. But with the modern technique of "riding the air" has come the need of greater control of the skis and this has lead, even on the big hills, to the use of lighter skis. *Weight*

197

The weight of the skis will, of course, vary with the stockiness and strength of the skier, but the following weights will be about right for average jumpers:

5′6″	7 to 9 lbs.	(weight per pair without bindings)
6′	8 to 10 lbs.	
6′6″	9 to 11 lbs.	
7′	10 to 12 lbs.	
7′6″	11 to 13 lbs.	
7′9″	12 to 14 lbs.	
8′	13 to 15 lbs.	
8′5″	14 to 16 lbs.	

Flexibility

A modern jumping ski is as carefully designed as most good downhill skis. They are long but not stiff. Flexibility, it has been found, is desirable in taking up the shock of landing. Flexibility and camber, of course, must vary with the weight of the rider.

Wood

Most jumping skis are multilaminated, for hickory is a precious item and solid hickory skis deemed to be an extravagance. But hickory is a remarkable wood, having spring and resilience and toughness beyond any other ski wood. Jumping skis should, therefore, have a preponderance of hickory and, if not a plastic base, then the bottom must be entirely of hickory.

Plastic (Kofix and Celolix) bottoms are just invading the jumping world. Within a few years they, or some other plastic with a low coefficient of friction, will be universally used (as will downhill waxing techniques). But such specialized bases come high and are needed only by good competition jumpers. Skiers in the beginning and intermediate stages will do well enough to stick to the old-fashioned wood skis on which lacquer and wax provide a good running surface.

Metal jumping skis, similar to those popular with recreational downhill skiers, have also made their advent. Doubtless in the end they will be perfected and used by many good jumpers. As their cost at present runs well over a hundred dollars, they cannot be recommended generally.

Boots

Jumping boots need to be both flexible and light. A stiff pair of downhill boots makes it impossible for the jumper to get a proper lean from the ankles in the air, nor can he make a good take-off or landing. The better the downhill boot the worse it will be for jumping.

For children their normal downhill boots are all right with the top hole or two left unlaced.

198

There are some inexpensive downhill boots (having flexibility forward but good lateral strength) which are ideal for jumping. They run about $15 to $18. And there are special jumping boots. Some compromises can be accepted; if the downhill boot has a sole that is not too stiff, and a good upper, then by unlacing the top two or three holes one can get a satisfactory flexion at the ankles. Such boots will serve on jumps up to 30 meters. But for anything longer, for any skier beyond the beginning stages, only good jumping boots can be recommended.

Bindings

Must be freely flexible. The sole of the boot should extend less than a half inch beyond the toe plates when the plate is properly mounted.

Jumping bindings, as used universally today, are the old-fashioned toe plates with a cable and forward-throw attachment. Some use the springs forward, but many prefer the sense of "live tension" which comes with the spring around the heel.

As the jumper must have great range of motion forward, both in the foot and at the ankle, it is essential that the downpull lug be as far forward as possible. Under the middle of the toe plate is about right. The better the jumper—the more accustomed he is to riding the air—the more "loose" will be his bindings. They should not, however, be so loose as to snap off at the heel upon landing!

If with your boots and bindings you can flex your knees until they almost touch the skis, you have achieved a good range of motion. There has been much talk about "unlaced boots." We doubt that this is necessary or desirable. It represents, rather, an unsolved problem in the design of boots and bindings.

Placing a *wooden wedge* or a *pad of sponge rubber* on the ski under the heel (with a lift of ½ to ¾") is often helpful in easing the forward flexion of the ankle.

Jumping Pants, Sweaters, Toques

These are so standard as to require no description. The point worth making is that neat, tight-fitting clothes give a certain zest to the sport. It does something irrational, but good to your morale. Needless to say the judges, too, are creatures of habit and tradition. In competition the skier is inevitably rated by what the judges expect to see.

Equipment for Cross-Country Skiing

Modern cross-country racing is a dash stretched out over several kilometers. That is to say light skis, light clothes, light boots, light poles are essential to light-footed techniques. Sheer strength and endurance do not now count more than speed techniques. And to provide for such running, modern courses are groomed and leveled, packed and set with a track, in a fashion unheard of twenty years ago.

International racers run on skis as carefully made as a violin and almost as delicate. Their boots are specially made for running and are scarcely higher than Oxfords. Their bindings pinion them only by the tips of the toes. Their knickers and parka are made from the lightest poplin. They run barehanded in reasonable weather, and bareheaded.

Since such skiers are few in number and expert in the matter of equipment, there is little use in attempting to describe what they already know.

But there is still the large population of high-school skiers who run for the "sake of the team," who have learned little technique and think racing is only a matter of bulling it through to the end of the course. Some guidance may be helpful to them:

Skis need not be expensive and should not be too delicate. Laminated cross-country skis ranging in price from $25 to $35 are plenty good enough. Beginners will find that a satisfactory running ski can be made from old downhill skis, edges taken off and the ski planed to a width of approximately 2⅛″ at the foot. Downhill skis which have a plastic base cannot be used as it is essential to have bare wood if one is to wax properly for cross-country.

The length of cross-country skis is not very different than that of slalom or combination skis: for the average racer 210 centimeters (6 feet 11 inches) will be about right. The stiffness and camber, of course, must vary with the weight of the runner; the main purpose of both stiffness and camber is to get a running surface which will allow the wax to grip over its full length and so distribute the carrying and the wearing. Generally speaking the stiffness and camber will be about right if the skis, gripped with maximum force between fingers and thumb, will just come together evenly along the running surface.

The regions of flexibility are important. The forward area of flexibility should extend from the turned-up tip back about 15 inches, and this should bend uniformly with pressure but not show weakness. If the extent of this flexible area in the ski is more than 15 inches, the ski will tend not to track well over bumps. The tail of the ski—the last 6 to 8 inches—should also be flexible so that the ski can ride down off bumps or over ditches without breaking. If the tails are properly designed, they will actually give the runner forward propulsion coming off a bump.

Bindings   There are several kinds of "rat-trap" bindings on the market, of which the Rottefeller and Rottefeller Snabb are the most common. They pin the boot down only at the very tip, allowing maximum flexibility in the toes for running. Such bindings are undoubtedly the best.

200

But they must be treated with care: all the thrust of going around corners must necessarily come on four little pins caught in the sole of the boot. A hard-twisting, clumsy wrench is enough to tear these pins out and ruin the running shoes.

Where the bindings should be mounted is open to considerable unimportant debate. Generally the runner will do very well if he mounts his bindings directly over the balance point of the ski. Thus the pivot point for the front-throw arm comes exactly on top of the balance point. The boot, of course, must be properly centered laterally so that it will carry the weight of the runner easily, just as with a racing skate.

Boots

Light boots you will have to buy. A light pair of downhill boots will never serve for cross-country. The soles are too stiff and the boots too heavy. In the end, you should fit yourself out with good running boots. They are quite inexpensive. As with downhill so with cross-country, a good boot is more important than a good ski.

For racing individual events the lighter the ski the better. However, if you are one of a team of four running in a relay race, you would be well advised to use something a little stouter and more sure to bring you home.

Poles: Do not be deluded by the notion that the longer the pole the better you will climb. Long poles throw your arms too high for effective pushing and are apt to drag on the return. Poles that reach to your armpits when you are standing on a floor are only a little bit short. A good average for most runners is 55 to 57 inches. Poles should be made of light, strong cane; the baskets need only be large enough to hold on packed snow. A large basket is heavy and clumsy and not noticeably better in soft snow than a small one. Tape the cane in between the nodes for added strength.

Touring Skis

Touring skis are the old man's best friend and the individualist's last resort. They are wider and more rugged than cross-country skis but not nearly as heavy as downhill skis. They have bare wood bottoms for waxing. The bindings are like jumping bindings rather than racing bindings, and commonly there is an extra "downpull lug" fastened back at the instep to give proper control over long or tricky downhill sections.

It is desirable to put a few feet of steel edge on both sides under the foot. Occasionally the tourer will run into hard ice or sun-burnished crust where the grip of the edges is the only thing that makes the slope skiable.

Waxing is the same as for cross-country racing. In some cases seal-skins or a cheap substitute made of plush can be used profitably on long uphill climbs although good cross-country runners would scorn lugging anything so heavy when wax will do almost as well.

Boots are any full comfortable flexible boots, old boots too soft for downhill skiing but rugged enough and warm enough to be suitable for the changing conditions you get in touring.

Aluminum tip: While the full paraphernalia of the touring skier or ski mountaineer will not be described here, all touring men should surely have in their pack a spare aluminum tip in case a ski is broken.

On Running Ski Races

Few, if any, sporting events are more difficult to put on than ski races. Weather is always in control. You may have laid out a fine, fast cross-country course, packed it well and flagged it, only to find that a night of rain has washed it out, leaving ponds and running brooks and the racers committed to a struggle through slush. You may have planned a good slalom course only to have a rain and freeze-up leave you with a hillside that has to be drilled with maul and drill in order to hold poles. You may have a downhill course on which, the night before the race, two feet of new snow has been dumped, or a jump frozen so hard that steel edges will not cut it.

Yet this is the sport; the races must go on. Skiers are winter birds, used to rough weather. With some experience in running races, with a good staff of willing men and women, and with sufficient planning ahead for possible crises, you will be able to pull off your tournament. Few races have to be canceled if there is manpower and planning.

In all cases, whether the weather be favorable or terrible, you have two and only two prime objectives:
1. That the race course or jumping hill be *safe*.
2. That the race be put on without official or technical error so that the racers may feel that they ski against racers, not against rule books and ski lawyers.

Danger, of course, is relative, for skiing is bound to be hazardous to a degree. Yet danger, unreasonable danger, in races can be defined: the skier is perfectly willing to take the chance of falling on ice and bumps and hard-packed snow. But not into trees or rocks, not over cliffs, not into crowds, dogs, grandstands, ropes, hot-dog vendors, or station wagons.

The matter of official or technical error, however unintended, is as unnecessary as it is frustrating. A racer starts too soon and is not properly called back, or a checker fails to mark the passage of the skier, or a well-wisher shouts something at a gate and the slalom runner thinks it is the gatekeeper calling him back, or a jumper hits a dog—these things and a thousand others can go wrong and, with sufficient lack of preparation on the part of the officials, certainly will. Once the mistake has been committed there is no way to rectify it. Disqualify the skier? Give him another run? Neither will fulfill the equal conditions for all racers demanded by fair competition.

For the benefit of those charged with the responsibility of running races, and to assist those who have not had much experience, we have prepared these *check lists of personnel and equipment* which are essential in every ski race.

The first thing to have is the proper rule book, in its latest edition. Most rules now are based on the F. I. S. standards set forth in two excellent booklets, one for alpine events, one for nordic. These may be obtained for $1.50 each at your divisional headquarters or from the United States Ski Association office (currently at Broadmore Hotel, Colorado Springs, Colorado). There are also U. S. S. A. rules, intercollegiate rules (N.C.A.A.), divisional rules, interscholastic rules.

Alpine Ski Races

PERSONNEL

1 Chief of race (in charge of the entire meet)
1 Course setter and assistant
1 Chief of course (responsible for course preparation)
1 Chief of timing and calculation (plus assistants)
1 Chief gatekeeper
Gatekeepers (each having no more than 4 gates to tend)
Shovelers, rakers, trampers, as needed
1 Chief starter (usually at bottom, giving the start over a telephone to the top)
1 Starter and assistant (at top)
1 Recorder and assistants (at finish)
1 Chief of communications and assistants
Police (as needed to keep spectators off course)
First-aid or medical man
1 Bib taker (in charge of giving out and picking up number bibs)
2 to 4 "Forerunners"
1 Referee (sometimes with assistants at start and finish)
1 Press officer (if needed)
Couple of "trouble shooters" and substitute gatekeepers
Ticket takers

EQUIPMENT

Rule books
Measuring tape (an "argument settler" for questionable gates)
Numerous starting lists

Clipboards
2 sets of 3 stop watches (synchronized before race)
Warming box for watches
Number bibs
Telephone communications (with auxiliary lines and a 2-way radio in
    reserve if warranted)
P. A. System (for all announcements)
Megaphone or sound-powered megaphone (at start)
Flags and poles; starting and finish gates
Small flags (to mark out areas likely to be difficult in bad weather)
Metronome for starter (if he cannot keep a good rhythmical count)
Shovels, rakes
Bluing (to mark positions of gates)
Salt and snow cement
Crowbar and sledge hammer
Scoring tables
Toboggan and first-aid equipment
Hot coffee and cocoa (at finish)
Ropes to keep spectators back
Prizes (ordered well in advance of race)

Downhill Races and Giant Slalom

Chief dangers: Rocks, stumps, trees, spectators in the path of potential
                falls.
                A narrow steep course.
                Insufficient room to stop at finish.
Main Difficulties: Communications breakdown.
                Deep soft snow or too little snow.

SLALOM RACES

Chief dangers: Hardwood poles (dowels) that shiver and splinter when
                broken.
                Spectators.
Main difficulties: An exact start.
                Well-trained gatekeepers.
                Communications.

Downhill Races

*Setting
the
Course*

Downhill races are supposed to be tests of skill, courage and endurance at very high speeds. They can be nightmares of physical peril, which only brute stupidity would lay out and call a race.

It follows therefore that the *course-setter* must be a man of experience and good judgment, a notable racer himself, for only such a man can see in the terrain its interesting possibilities and its inherent dangers: how far a man will ride off a bump, how fast he will come out of a turn, how much his skis will drift on a fast fall-away corner, where control gates will be seen in time to check the skier and guide him away from an unreasonable hazard.

Just as the speed and take-off must be set to suit the best jumper in the field, so the downhill course must be set so that all competitors can get through it, but only the best ones at full speed. The course must suit the field of skiers present; it will be a very different course for high-school runners than for B-class skiers and still more difficult for top intercollegiate or international racers.

Most physical hazards can be eliminated by the proper use of control gates and course police. Yet it must be said that control gates wrongly placed serve only to increase the danger. They are much worse than no controls at all.

There are courses and conditions when even control gates do not offer reasonable safety. Sometimes safety nets can then be strung out on stout poles to keep racers from falling into rocks or trees or over cliffs. Such nets may be life-saving—and yet one wonders whether this is not the time when the race itself should be called off, whatever its importance.

A good course-setter, who knows racing, will want to:
1. Use plenty of control gates.
2. Use the bumps and hollows of the hill with imagination but yet be sure that even the most reckless young skier will not out-jump or out-fall his landing area.
3. Ski the course several times, fast, to be sure the control gates are in the right place and visible well in advance.
4. Use many small flags in a line to direct the skier toward the "line" or the controls in the event of fog or falling snow.

A good downhill course should include a fast start, high-speed turns, large knolls where pre-jumping is called for and followed by ample landing areas, schusses where small bumps and speed must be dealt with. A fine course will also have sections which may be run safely without checking, but which are often run faster with just the right degree of checking. At the *finish area* there should be a roped-off space long and broad enough to permit the racer to make his swing and stop.

This may be the easiest or the most difficult of jobs. If the weather has been kind to you, the racers training on the course have broken it

Preparing the Course

205

out and packed it hard, leaving you only the job of setting the controls (if any are necessary) and running the race.

On the other hand, you may be dealing with old gray ice, iron-bound ruts, moguls, bare ground. Or your problem may be too much soft snow dumped on you a day or two in advance of the race. Here the best solution is *boot-tramping*. It may seem slow, arduous work, but in the end you will have a proper base, hard all the way through.

Special attention must be given to the *landing surfaces below long jumps or fall-away corners*. They must be packed wide and hard, first by boot-tramping, then packed smooth.

The Start

The starting area of a course should be a flat or nearly flat area where the skier can approach the line without having to hold himself back at great effort with his poles. Just beyond the starting line the slope should break down steeply so that, with a couple of good thrusts of his poles, the skier will have gained good speed.

Other than failure of the telephone system, the biggest cause for distemper among racers is a poor method of starting. Many methods have been tried; the rule books annually come out with modifications.

The following system, however, will generally give satisfactory results and is recommended:
1. The chief starter remains at the bottom of the course having the master watch to go by and standing near the timers so that they can hear his count. He is in communication with the starter at the top by means of a telephone.
2. The starter at the top holds his telephone so that the racer, the assistant starter, and he can all hear the count.
3. The assistant starter stands in front of the racer and to one side, facing uphill, with one hand gently "stiff-arming" the shoulder of the racer.
4. When the course is ready, the forerunners gone, the time for starting on hand, the chief starter gives the count in a clear loud voice. "10 seconds ... 5 ... 4 ... 3 ... 2 ... 1 ... Go!" He must give the count in a *steady and exact rhythm,* which will be the same for each second and for each racer. If he is unsure in his rhythm a Metronome will help.
5. Subsequent racers are started in the same way at minute intervals.
6. If a racer is not on hand for his start, and has not sufficient excuse, he is disqualified, but his place left blank, rather than having the next man move up as this can cause confusion in calculations later on.
7. If a racer jumps the gun (if his *feet* cross the line ahead of the count), the starter must call *at once* in a *loud voice,* "Back! Back! Back!"

The racer must then come back and again put both feet across the starting line or face disqualification. He need not put his tips across.

8. The referee in charge of start is the disinterested official who is there to make sure the start is given properly and the call of "Back" sufficiently loud to be heard by a premature starter.

Keeping Spectators off the Course

Mention has already been made of the importance of keeping the finish area clear so that racers, tired and relaxed, may swing to an easy stop. But the same problem exists throughout the course, especially in the critical areas where the wildest spills may occur and most spectacular skills in skiing are to be demonstrated. Most spectators do not actually wish to be killed by a skier, or to kill one. Yet sometimes the calls are breath-takingly close. The main trouble comes from the fact that the spectator (unless he be a racer) has no idea of the speed and momentum which the racer must control under the trying circumstances of a big jump or a long schuss or a cataract of bumps. The skier is riding his line to the inch; all his calculations are based on the supposition of a clear course ahead. He is already pushing himself to the limit to hold his line (otherwise it would not be the proper line). The crowding in of spectators can be enough to throw him off that line and perhaps result in a disastrous mistake.

An Injury on the Course

This is one of these tense and unavoidable problems for which a good ski patrol, highly trained and coolly operating, is absolutely essential. If a man is badly injured in the middle of the worst section of the course, only heroic measures, backed with great skill and efficiency, can save the situation. The man may be right on the skiers' "line." He may be invisible to the next competitor. No amount of shouting or flag-waving will divert the on-coming racer. The ski patrol has less than a minute to get out on the course, roll an injured man onto a toboggan (being careful of a back or neck injury) and get him out of the trajectory of the next skier.

Slalom

Slalom races are technically the hardest ski events to put on. They require the largest numbers of trained and experienced officials. They demand a degree of devotion and competence on the part of the "gatekeepers" beyond that of any of the other events. More things can go wrong in a slalom—and often do—than in any other sporting event. For all that, a well-run race is a beautiful and exciting spectacle and well worth the effort.

Course-setter

Only a good slalom skier, and a man with some further experience in setting courses, can get the most out of the terrain features of a particular hill. Good slalom courses are not set "by the book," with an attempt somehow to fit in all the combinations of gates shown on the printed page. They are, rather, tailored to the slope, making for an interesting variety of flag combinations, utilizing the available bumps and hollows, and yet always maintaining the fluid nature of good skiing. The man who has a "feel" for setting a good course does so because he can "feel" how it will be to ski it.

Course Preparation

Gray ice and deep new snow offer the only physical obstacles to running a slalom race. Falling snow, fog, even rain may cause discomfort, but do not rule out slalom. In the case of deep new snow, as with the downhill, *boot-tramping* is the best answer. If necessary, more than once. A slalom course must be hard. Boot-tramping is most effective if the base has a chance to harden overnight. On some occasions, when faced with cold powdery snow, a careful seeding of the area with rock salt may help harden the loose snow.

Ice is trying, but usually need not cause the cancellation of the race. Salt is not recommended except in extreme cases. A thorough hacking with the sides of ski boots will usually start the loosening-up process; when this is followed by side stepping the course, a usable surface will result. A fairer slalom race can be run on ice than on powder.

In the case of slush, if the snow is so slow as to be torture for the racers, you can add some "snow cement" just before the race and expect it to harden up the slalom surface for a few hours. Snow cement is a tricky chemical. It should be practiced with before trusting it on a slalom course.

Poles

The greatest hazard in a slalom race is undoubtedly the use of *hardwood dowels for poles*. These murderous substitutes have nothing to recommend them and it is hard to see why they are still in use in some slalom races in this country. Such dowels tend to splinter when hit and become lances flailing down the slope. A racer may knock a pole out, breaking it and sending it ahead of him down the slope, only to find as it goes end over end that it sticks into the snow, sharpened up, ready to impale him.

Skiers have been skewered and killed by accidents no more complicated than this.

208

Instead of hardwood poles, use stout bamboo, or bamboo wrapped with fiber glass, for slalom poles. Good slalom poles can be cut from young green hardwood saplings (with care taken to cut all branches smooth). The poles should be eight feet long or longer.

The start is substantially the same as that described for downhill races, except that in the case of slalom there must be absolute co-ordination between the chief starter, who makes the starting count over the phone, and the timers, nearby at the finish.

The Start

The *chief starter must be able to maintain an exact rhythm in his count.* Slaloms are won by split seconds; it is only natural that the racers will be timing their starts to the finest shaving of a second. The slightest variation in the count—5 . . . 4 . . . 3 . . . 2 . . . 1 . . . Go!—will cause false starts, or delayed starts, and bring down the just wrath of skiers and coaches on the race committee.

Gatekeepers

Of all the unsung heroes of slalom, there are none compared to the gatekeepers. They stand for hours at their stations, in freezing weather, keeping their section of the course, unable to enjoy more than a fragment of the race, resetting poles, stamping out ruts, keeping spectators back, taking abuse from coaches.

The gatekeeper has one primary job: to see that both feet of every competitor cross the imaginary line running between both poles of each gate. If not, that skier is disqualified. *There are no penalties* any more; either the skier makes it or he is out. *The burden of responsibility rests, not with the gatekeeper, but with the skier.* The gatekeeper is not permitted to shout after the skier that he has missed a gate. The skier himself, if in doubt, must stop and ask, or risk disqualification.

When so asked, the gatekeeper replies either "Back" or "Go on." That is all.

Secondarily, the gatekeeper is responsible for maintaining his gates, replacing broken poles, stamping out dangerous ruts, skidding away heavy accumulations of snow.

General rules concerning gatekeepers might be as follows:
1. Place only competent people in this important job, and then back them up.
2. Place your best gatekeepers at the critical sections of the course.
3. Have them well briefed on the latest rules.
4. No gatekeeper should be asked to patrol more than 4 gates.
5. Have them out and ready at their stations a half hour before time for the start of the race.
6. See that they, too, get coffee, and leave a few substitute gatekeepers ready to go in and give relief if the weather is cold.

No one—including both skiers and coaches—is as likely to be right in the case of a disputed disqualification as the gatekeeper, who is in the best position to observe what happened.

Flag Combinations

Having previously stated that a good slalom course is tailored to the potentialities of the particular hill, we do not propose to create an encyclopedia of flag patterns which ingenious course-setters have worked out over the last thirty years. The F.I.S. rule book has several score of them carefully illustrated. It is not the art (or diabolical skill) with which a particular group of gates is placed which counts; it is the continuity with which the whole course is laid out top to bottom.

A few of the basic patterns, however, ought to be mentioned for those who want to learn slalom racing and course-setting. Begin simply. Avoid complex arrangements and think of motion rather than gates. Start with simple open gates in an S-shaped sequence. Learn to use the terrain features you have rather than to lay out combinations that bear no sensible relation to the ground and snow of your hill.

1. Gates may be set to tempt the skier to go too fast.
2. Gates may be set slow, to see whether he knows how to maintain his speed.
3. Gates may be set which require absolute precision throughout a complex sequence of motions.
4. Gates may be set which give the skier alternative routes and force him to choose for himself, matching his skill and judgment against the course-setters' plan.
5. And gates, God knows! may be set in such a manner that no skier can get through.

The above are the most common flag patterns. You can readily see the kind of primitive problems they present the racer. Now test them in close relation to the terrain:

1. Try these gates in relation to a good-sized bump: on top of the bump, in front of the bump, to each side of the bump, below the bump. Here are five more variables already.
2. Next test them with gullies, steep pitches, flats, in the same way.
3. Then see how the problem changes when the flags are set obliquely on the hill, or are offset from each other, or are staggered.
4. Lastly place them in such a way that the skier is led into the sequence too fast; or must come out fast.

After you have come to know these simple patterns of flags in a variety of ways, it is time to consider setting a whole slalom course where many combinations and many variables are at your disposal. Can the expert skier maintain his speed and rhythm? Does the overanxious beginner go too fast? Or have you produced a conglomeration of jerky, hectic "sets," which seem to be more or less independent of one another.

A good rule to follow is to set the top few gates and the last few in a fast, rhythmical, uncomplicated manner.

When you have mastered all this, you will already be a fine course-setter. The "Oslo's," "E's," and "Reverse Seelos'" will seem easy enough to use when the appropriate time and terrain is on hand.

Giant Slalom

The problems of both downhill races and of slalom are combined in this race and so need no further comment here.

Ski Jumping

CHIEF DANGERS

The approach to the take-off
The dip and outrun

MAIN DIFFICULTIES

A soft landing hill or an icy dip
Falling snow or gusty winds

PERSONNEL

1 Chief of race (in charge of entire jumping meet)
1 Chief of hill (in charge of conditioning the hill, setting speed and take-off, etc.)
1 Starter or flagman (on the knoll where he can see the entire hill; he signals the jumpers when the hill and the judges are ready, or holds up the meet when the hill needs fixing)
1 Assistant starter (at top)
1 Announcer
2 Certified jumping judges (3, or even 5, in important meets)
1 Recorder (taking down distance scores and style points and computing total scores. He will require one or more assistants)
10 to 30 distance markers (depending on the size of the hill)
4 to 20 trampers with steel-edged skis (some on the knoll and the rest below near the transition, where they can go out quickly and tramp down)
Rake and shovel men
First-aid and medical men
1 person in charge of giving out and collecting the number bibs
Referee
Police as required to keep spectators back
Ticket takers and other assistants
3 to 6 "Forejumpers"

EQUIPMENT

Rule books

Measuring tape or chain

Fishpoles for marking distance

Clipboards

4 Starting lists (for recorder, announcer, starter and bib man)

Number bibs

Megaphone, sound-powered megaphone, or P.A. system

Shovels, rakes, baskets

Spruce boughs or bluing (for take-off and dip, especially in flat light or falling snow)

Salt (if dealing with hard ice)

Toboggan and first-aid equipment

Distance-conversion tables (suited to your hill)

Scoring tables

Combined-result tables if a combined-event meet

Ribbons and prizes (ordered at least a month in advance!)

The above list of personnel and equipment is sufficient for almost any meet. On small hills the arrangements can be much simplified. On larger jumping hills you need more distance markers and further division of responsibility: another starter way at the top, a man in charge of the take-off, a man in charge of the condition of the dip and outrun, more trampers, etc. etc.

Also, on a larger hill, a P.A. system and a good telephone system are necessary. It is essential here that the chief of hill (stationed in the judges' stand, probably) be able to talk directly to the starter at the top of the inrun, the man on the take-off, the man on the knoll, the man in the dip, and to the head judge, if need be. However the labor be divided up, from the skiers' point of view, the man on the knoll (the flagman) is the essential person and should be an experienced jumper. When he flags them down, they *know* that the hill is ready and the track clear.

Danger Areas in Ski Jumping: The approach to the take-off, the dip, and the first part of the outrun are the danger areas on any jumping hill, small or large. They deserve your special attention during practice and during tournaments.

Soft Landing: The greatest danger facing the jumper is a soft landing. Provided the dip were good, a jumper could land on a mound of beer bottles and tin cans more safely than on a soft hill.

The most common trouble comes from letting the hill go unprepared too long. There are clubs which, almost by the compulsion of a tradition, leave fixing the jumping hill until the day before, or the night before, or the morning before a scheduled tournament.

Sometimes, however, the race committee is faced with a heavy fall of snow the day before the tournament. In their hurry to get the hill in shape, they will simply send a few men out to pack it with jumping skis. This gives a surface hardness which is deceptive, for jumping skis are too big and long to successfully compact the snow. The hill looks fine, however, smooth and beautiful, and the first few jumpers ride all right. Then, about a third of the way through the tournament, the shell begins to break down and rut out into a deep groove. At this point there is nothing to do. Stamping cannot help. The snow is too powdery. A groove is bad enough to land in, but to fill it up with soft snow would be much worse. So the meet goes on, even though bad spills are bound to result.

There is only one thing to do in this situation: before the meet *boot-tramp the whole landing, dip, and first part of the outrun.* Trample it hard, then rake it, pack it with downhill skis, and let it set.

If done a day or so before the tournament, a perfect hill will result.

New Snow the Day of the Tournament: If faced with a heavy fall of snow the night before, or the morning before, the tournament, there is not time to compact it. The only thing to do is to rake and shovel the snow off the inrun, landing and transition and then pack what remains with downhill skis.

Damp New Snow: This is the bane of all ski jumpers. The trouble is that damp new snow compacts into a porcelain-hard glazy surface. It will not hold a track on the inrun, and the dip and outrun become both icy and rutted. Repeated tramping and raking will help it (though the take-off will constantly delay your tournament and make the jumpers worried), but by far the best thing is to rake and shovel the damp new snow off completely, down to the old hard snow which, whether damp or cold, will be good to jump on.

Icy Conditions: It is rare to have a hill so icy that ski boots won't cut into it. In other words, often all that needs to be done is to send some men out to boot-tramp and rake the inrun and hill, after which a little fresh snow thrown on will make a perfect landing surface.

When true "glare ice" occurs, on the inrun and where the jumpers have been landing (as a result of jumping during a thaw) then you must resort to *salt.* You seed the upper inrun and the landing hill with rock salt and give it a little time to work. The steep parts of the hill are boot-tramped. Then fresh snow is thrown on, sometimes mixed with a little more salt, and the whole surface worked down and packed. It will freeze hard overnight and make a perfect jumping hill where the day before the jump looked like a back-yard glacier.

There is some danger in using salt. If you get too much on, the snow will turn mushy. If you put it on the take-off and dip, and more is brought down from above, these areas will be relatively slower than the rest of the hill. About 10 pounds of salt are sufficient to fix a 20-meter hill.

Sloppy Wet Snow: Sometimes a warm rain or a May-day-come-three-months-early will turn a good jumping hill into running water. Even then it can be used and good jumps result if the jumpers know how to paint on their waxes in steps as the downhill boys do.

High Winds, Snowstorms: It may happen—as it rarely does—that the only thing to do under these conditions is to postpone or call off your jumping meet.

Judging: Form and Distance

Judges are a law unto themselves and, for a brief period each winter weekend, the lords of all they survey. The jumper must not only seek to make the longest jumps, he must also please the judges (or flatter their prejudices, in some cases) by the way he performs. There is no escaping this; in jumping, points are awarded for form equally with distance. Moreover every sanctioned meet must have its quota of certified judges.

Judges look for many details, but inevitably their reaction is based upon the whole "feel" of the jump: the poise, the courage, the control the jumper exhibits, from the time he starts down the inrun until he is safely out on the flat.

Judges look for:
    a strong take-off, perfectly timed,
    grace and confidence in the air,
    quick recovery from minor imperfections,
    and a sure, smooth landing.

For each jump each judge has a maximum of 20 points he can award. Since 20 points signify a perfect jump in all respects, it is rare indeed that any jumper gets such a mark. Anything above 16.5 or 17 points is excellent. Distance and form count equally.

Three jumps, two to score: When time permits, when your field of jumpers is not too large, the fairest way is to give each jumper three competitive jumps and score him on the best two. Thus a slip on the take-off, or one badly timed jump, or one fall will not completely eliminate a good jumper.

Cross-Country Races

CHIEF DANGERS:

Downhill sections too steep, narrow, icy or soft for fast running

214

MAIN DIFFICULTIES:

Insufficient tramping of a track. Insufficient flagging for fast running

PERSONNEL:

Chief of race

Course-setter and assistants

Head timer and assistants

Starter and assistant

Recorder and assistants

Checkers (at strategic points along the course)

Head of communications and transportation

Bib taker (with number bibs)

Referee

First-aid or medical man

3 to 6 "Forerunners"

2 "Postrunners"

Police as needed at road crossings, etc.

Feeding-station personnel

EQUIPMENT:

Rule books

Watches (synchronized, and equipped with interval hands for multiple
finishes)

Plenty of small flags (use a special warning color to indicate the approach of a difficult part of course)

Starting lists (for starters, recorders, checkers, etc.)

Megaphone or P.A. system

Start and finish flags

Toboggan and first-aid equipment (available by car)

Hot coffee and cocoa (available at finish)

Waxing room and showers available nearby

Feeding stations (in long races, oranges, sugar water, tea, etc.)

Scoring tables, conversion tables, combined tables

Communications with key points out on course

Ribbons and prizes (ordered well in advance)

Running Cross-Country Races

| High-school races | 3 to 5 miles |
| Intercollegiate races | 8 to 10 miles |

International races:
| Relay | 4 runners, 10 kilometers each |

15 kilometer combined cross-country

15 kilometer special cross-country

30 kilometer special cross-country
50 kilometer special cross-country

Cross-country races are relatively easy to lay out and conduct. With reasonable planning and foresight they offer little difficulty. Weather to some extent controls the race, but in general a good race can be run in any kind of weather, provided the organization is sufficient.

Laying Out the Course: There should be much variety in the terrain: bump running, woods running, downhill sections, short uphill climbs, at least one long uphill climb, and clear going all the way. The purpose of the race is to test technique under a variety of skiable conditions. Steep downhill sections through brush or thick spruce cover, barbed-wire fences to climb over, farmers' dogs to fight off, brooks, ice, rocks, bare roads may suit the sadistic temperament of some coursesetters, but they are not legitimate obstacles in a cross-country race.

Modern rules specify that the races shall begin and end at the same elevation, from a spectator's point of view from the same point. The rules also give maximums and minimums for total uphill climbing, depending upon the nature of the race, and indicate that the longest single climb should not be at the very beginning, or the very end, but somewhere in the middle or beginning of the last third of the course. It is common practice for clubs to run two laps of the same course; this permits the course work to be cut in half and tends to increase the excitement of the race.

In no case make a figure-eight type of course, where one track crosses another. Great confusion results, checkers are apt to be balled up as to who went where, and unintentional "short cuts" can occur.

Preparing the Course: A good course is wide, packed hard, and has a good track (about 8 inches wide) set in it. Packing the course should begin several days before the race, ideally weeks before the race. If there are icy downhill stretches, this gives time to lay out a less dangerous alternative route. If there is deep snow, perhaps wind-blown to breakable crust, the course should be packed first by snowshoers going three abreast, followed by packers on skis.

Flags: There are almost never enough flags used. No one but an active cross-country racer can imagine how fast a good skier will come along the course, how quickly he will plunge into a wooded or sharp downhill section, how easy it is for him to "run by" a track turning abruptly to one side.

Flags have two purposes:
1. They mark the course. The skier should always be able to see flags ahead of him. Fifty yards ahead is none too long for a good runner.

2. They warn him of sudden changes or dangerous spots ahead, sharp downhill pitches, sudden corners, ice, roads, brooks.

For general purposes a bright orange flag on a short pole, or a strip of orange bunting or crepe paper tied to branches is sufficient. The warning flags should be of another color, placed close together within reasonable distance of the change of course or unusual obstacle.

Maps: It is helpful to the racers to have a contour map prepared of your course so that they may study it. It is also a good thing to make a profile of the climbs, flats, and downhill stretches.

Checkers: At key points along the course there must be checkers to make sure that all racers pass each station and to lend a hand in case some inexperienced runner arrives in a state of exhaustion. Such checking stations are usually placed out at the critical points and on the promontories of the course so as to discourage any attempt to "short cut" the course. The stations should be clearly shown on the map, as a further guide to the runner in how much of the course is left to run.

Feeding Stations: In any long race at least one feeding station is desirable out on the course. Warm tea (not hot), sugar water, and a section of orange are commonly supplied to racers who want them. For sparkling results let a pretty girl tend your feeding station.

Starting: The start is usually given at minute intervals, although with a large field (and when the track is sufficiently wide to be safe) it is all right to use half-minute intervals. In the case of a relay race, all teams must start their first men at the same time and on the same line.

General Rules: No attempt will be made here to paraphrase the rule books, but some understanding of the essential rules is desirable:

1. A skier must complete the entire course, on skis, and without assistance.
2. 'On skis' means he must run all parts of the course on skis.
3. 'On skis' also means he must complete the course with at least one of his original skis. In case of a broken ski, he may accept one ski from a spectator but not both. He may, however, accept poles as fast as he breaks them.
4. 'Without assistance' means without physical or technical help. He may, for example, stop and accept a tube of wax from a bystander or coach, but he must clean his skis and apply the wax himself.
5. The overtaking skier has the right of way. When the skier actually overtakes the man ahead (not when he is fifty feet behind) he shouts "Track" and the man ahead is obliged to step out of the track and let the better runner past.

217

6. Of course no racer is allowed to detain or block or interfere with another racer. Neither can any spectator or coach actively assist or attempt to thwart one of the racers.

Forerunners, Postrunners: The most common weakness in a cross-
country race (other than insufficient flags) is in starting too few forerunners too late. In spite of everything the rule books say, and in spite
of all common sense, many races are still run with no one to break the
track for the racers. Sometimes, when snow is falling and especially
when the wind is drifting snow over the track, you may see the best
runner hopelessly bogged down, breaking trail for the rest of the pack.
Curses and protests cannot help. The race is a miserable failure right
from the start. It is such negligence as this which gives cross-country
racing its dour reputation.

Therefore, be sure there are enough forerunners, starting early
enough to keep the track fair for everyone.

Postrunners are needed, too, to run the course, to tell the checkers
to head home, and be sure that there is no exhausted or injured competitor straggling along toward an abandoned finish line.

Training and Exercises

Sigmund Ruud once said: "Downhill men train on beer, cross-
country runners train on snuss, and jumpers train on 'hop-kake.'" Jumping cake had more value than silver cups: Sigmund was really talking
about the fun of skiing. He could laugh at the alleged differences
among skiers because he knew all events, was a fine downhill runner,
and at the time the best jumper in the world. Training was not a "program" for him. It would never have occurred to him to be "out of
shape" in any season of the year.

Skiing is a strenuous sport. Good competitive skiers have to be
athletes. But the athletes know how to train; this section is not for them.
It is not a monograph on kinesthetics and body building. We will not
write an outline of calisthenics (that horrid word). We will not urge
the Wall Street junior executive to join a construction gang in order to
strengthen his snowplow. We want only to make a few general points
about conditioning.

Probably it is the intermediate and ambitious recreational skier,
over the age of thirty, who most needs to be encouraged to "train." He
may not be expecting to race against Toni Sailer or Buddy Werner, but
in fact he is already racing against age, weight, steam-heated houses,
office routines, the income tax, alcohol, long automobile trips; over
gray ice or deep new snow he may still be racing with dreams of glory
in his mind. The hospital lies in wait.

Training should be fun, and therefore not training at all but only a pleasant variety of sports intelligently mixed with special exercises. There is much to be said for the off-season sports. One can keep in shape and develop skiing skills without knowing it. The excitement of the game and the group nature of the activity drive the person harder than he would drive himself alone. A reasonable and varied program of sports is better than any haphazard alternation between overexercise and no exercise. And it is better than a strict and dogged routine of squat jumps and wall weights.

Good training is as much of the mind as of the body.

Training for skiing is no different, for the most part, than that proper for any rugged sport. First you must have the basic element—a *"good condition"* of the body. On top of that, and over a period of months, you can build up *strength and endurance*. On top of this you can work for *speed and timing,* quick decisions and quick reactions. And lastly you add certain *specialized skills* which apply to one or more of the ski events, should you ski in competition.

Americans, so far, have not gone in for summer ski jumping on plastic hills or for the soap-greased diving chutes we hear are employed in Europe. Our sports traditions tend to favor a reasonable alternation of the sport with the season. This is not necessarily bad. There are many sports which have a direct carry-over value in skiing, both endurance sports and speed sports.

For example: walking is probably the best general conditioner known. How many times a month do you take a 20-mile hike?

Beyond this, rugged outdoor work would be the conditioner of choice: work in the woods, farming, hard construction work would be ideal. Skiers who live this sort of life need only consider sports which give speedy reactions and accurate timing. But few skiers do live this way. The rest must plan their recreation more carefully so as to give themselves a balance of endurance sports and speed sports, and add to that the exercises necessary to build up where they are weak.

Training for strength and endurance
long-distance running and hiking, distance events in track
long-distance swimming
canoe camping
mountain climbing
soccer
crew
water polo

Training for speed and timing

    tennis
    squash
    diving
    trampoline and tumbling
    soccer
    volleyball
    broad jump, high jump, hurdles and dash events in track

In general it is easier to build up the big muscles of the legs and thighs than it is to build up the arms and shoulder girdles. Months must go into the strengthening of the legs, but strong arms and shoulders cannot be built up without years of work. Bar bells and wall weights can give special help when used regularly and intelligently, but they are no substitute for work or sports. Indeed, they can be overdone on two counts: first, they tend to emphasize one group of muscles and therefore to build up strength in a lopsided way; second, they are boring. Training is not just the piling up of muscle. An athlete can go stale from too much work and too little rest—or he can go stale from sheer boredom over an epic but stupid regime.

Certain off-season sports deserve special mention for their carry-over value to skiing: for slalom: tennis; for downhill: soccer; and for jumping: highboard diving, tumbling, trampoline.